Dancing with

The Mask

by

Sue Plumtree

First published in Great Britain in 2008 by

Lifelong Books
Flat 10
Floyer Close
Queens Road
Richmond TW10 6HS

www.sueplumtree.co.uk
www.plumtreementoring.co.uk

Designed by JAC, Crowborough, E. Sussex

Printed and bound in England by Biddles

ACKNOWLEDGEMENTS

First and foremost I want to thank Alan Bec, my life coach and friend who became the force that encouraged, guided, supported and stood by me – often in the face of much resistance – in the process of transforming my life. Without him this book would not have been written.

I would also like to thank my friend and editor, Shahrukh Husain. Without her whole-hearted support and encouragement this would have been a lesser book.

Thank you, too, to Zoe Meyer, who masterminded the project of bringing this book out and giving it all her love. The final product is evidence of it.

Philip Coulson, Photography, Isleworth deserves a special mention for producing such a flattering likeness.

Finally, I would like to thank all of you who touched my life, either fleetingly or deeply and lastingly. Thank you for helping me learn about myself, a process that goes on and on.

I dedicate this book to my Mum and Dad who provided me with the springboard from which I could re-create my life.

ABOUT THE AUTHOR

Sue Plumtree, FCIPD (Fellow of the Chartered Institute of Personnel and Development) was Personnel Manager at ActionAid, one of the leading third world development charities. For 13 years she ran her own training business specialising in business communication skills for managers. In 2000 she was awarded a Certificate in Higher Education, and worked as a Lecturer at Westminster Business School where she lectured young HR professionals.

She spent the next 8 years working at the Institute of Directors as a Client Development Executive before leaving to follow her heart. She is now a coach/mentor, writer and speaker.

Her first book *'Across A Crowded Room: How to Find and Keep the Love of Your Life'* (Hodder Headline) was published in 1995. Sue also facilitated her own *'Get On With Your Life'* series of courses and delivered her interactive series of talks *'Let's Talk About…'* in Richmond, Surrey, where she lives.

However, of greater importance and relevance, she says, is her willingness to be open to the richness of life's experiences, meeting them often – though by no means always – with grace and integrity, and with an unfailing readiness to learn from them.

INTRODUCTION

It was not until my feelings of sadness, loneliness and resentment became so intense and I was practically on my knees that I finally surrendered to the possibility that there might be another way.

As soon as I became willing to look at myself I began to see how I kept deceiving myself, oppressing myself, struggling, resisting and blaming, and how this caused me to create a life experience that was loveless, meaningless and empty.

Stopping all those self-defeating and self-destructive habits and behaviours was the beginning of a journey that turned out to be an experience so unique and profound that I feel compelled to share it as widely as possible. The most important thing I learned about how to create a fulfilling life was this: first change yourself and then everything else will follow.

I believe that the very fact that I was willing to do so enabled me to start noticing some of the myriad of things that happen all around me which I might otherwise have missed.

In the last few years I have dropped my socially acceptable mask, I have become more authentic, I have created a life that is deeply fulfilling as a coach/mentor, workshop facilitator and writer and I continue to attract into my life many wonderful people. More important to me is the fact that I have become clear about how I was able to do that. Along the way I have developed a set of beliefs and a series of tools that now form part of my teaching and the very foundation of my life. In turn, I have become privileged to witness many moments of insight and 'liberation' both on my courses and through my coaching.

This book is in two parts. Part 1 is an account of the forces that shaped me, that caused me to develop a personality that was intended to gain me approval and love. Although Part 1 examines my past I started writing it when I believed I had become fully self-aware and reached my goals. But as time went on, and I continued to feel isolated and disappointed I started recording everything that was happening to me as a way to try to understand why so little had changed. I had not anticipated that there would be a Part 2.

Part 2 became a moment-by-moment account of my inner struggles, the problems and challenges I met and how I dealt with them. It was only afterwards that I realised that Part 2 was a direct record of my journey towards authenticity, a journey that is on-going.

In this book I go deeply within myself which enabled me to develop a detailed roadmap of the inner processes of change and transformation as truthfully and emotionally open as I know how. This book will support and encourage you, the reader, to examine the role you play in the creation of your life and shows you how to transform your reality.

1

How my early upbringing shaped the person I became

I woke up one morning noticing, as I had more and more often lately, the tight knot in my stomach and a sense of unshed tears.

I tried to think of a time when I hadn't felt like that but couldn't. It was as if I had been feeling like this forever. I looked at my husband Jim who lay sleeping beside me, snoring gently and I felt nothing. I had to get ready for work but paused, trying to collect my thoughts, trying to work out why I felt like this.

All I ever wanted was to be loved or, to put it more accurately, all I ever wanted was to *feel* that I was loved. Instead, all I'm feeling is – what? Lonely? Empty? Disconnected? Yes, lonely most of all. I wondered, when did it all start?

Looking back to my childhood I recognized clearly, I think for the first time, that I had been groomed not only for loneliness but also to become a chameleon. Throughout my childhood and young womanhood my parents continually impressed upon me how important it was that I be liked and approved of. Today, I am also struck by the fact that, even though external circumstances forced my parents to take huge risks just to survive one of history's most turbulent periods, World War II and its aftermath, when it came to me, they tried to create an environment that was as safe and free of potential disappointments as possible. It was an upbringing that discouraged making mistakes, genuinely expressing my feelings, especially the so-called negative ones, learning to interact with others or taking responsibility. As a consequence I developed qualities that led me to create a life that was lonely, isolated and inauthentic. How did that come about?

The account of my journey highlights not only the obvious ways of trying to make myself appealing to others but also the darker unconscious forces (my Shadow) that drove me to sabotage myself again and again without realizing what I was doing.

I grew up a lonely child, not necessarily because that is how I was by nature but because my parents' fears, beliefs and background unintentionally fostered this state in me and shaped me in ways I only now began to understand.

I knew that my parents had wanted and loved me very much – sometimes I thought they loved me too much. I often felt stifled. The problem was that their own background and life experiences caused them to become overly protective of me.

Both had been brought up in middle-class families, a fact Papi in particular was very proud of and tried to drum into me.

"We are middle class", he would often say to me, "we are a better kind of people." I knew he was referring to our own neighbourhood whom he dismissively called "plebs." I never understood what it meant to be "better" than others nor how that sense of being "better" was supposed to be expressed, which frustrated Papi no end.

My parents were born in Central Europe, my mother, Mami, in Austria and my father, Papi, in Czechoslovakia. Papi was a respected journalist with the one German language newspaper in town and my Mum a dentist's assistant. Papi belonged to a circle of intellectual friends, artists and writers, holding debates and discussing life, the universe and everything. He regarded intellectual conversation as both stimulating and a way of life.

When my parents met it was love at first sight, a love that was true and real, and that lasted until the day he died. Mami thought Papi was a hero and looked up to him and he, in turn, idolized her.

Mami's schooling had been sporadic because her family had moved around a lot due to her father's job as a salesman. Papi's education, on the other hand, had been that of a middle class young man, graduating from University in 1928.

People enjoyed Papi's company. He was a popular conversationalist: articulate, informed, witty and entertaining – everything I was not, yet longed to be because that was, obviously, how one became popular.

Mami believed that too and, in the belief that she was acting selflessly, she encouraged me to spend as much time with him as possible convinced that anything he might say to me would be more useful than whatever she might say. Yet I know her behaviour – pushing me away from her and towards Papi – was prompted by love both for him and for me. Her efforts to put herself second to him also, unintentionally, made me see her in the same light she saw herself.

Only weeks after they met, Europe was thrown into turmoil by the arrival of Hitler. Papi, in his role of journalist, volunteered as a carrier of intelligence to and from the British Government and, as such, had advance information that he tried to use (despite the sworn secrecy of his assignments) to save the lives of family and friends. In most cases it was not to be. His warnings fell largely on deaf ears. I imagine that no-one could comprehend the enormity of what Papi was trying to tell them and so refused to believe him. My parents fled but most of our family members and friends were sent to concentration camps or executed.

They first aimed for Bolivia where they lived from 1939 to 1944. They knew nothing about Bolivia except that it was a safe place to hide from the holocaust that was burning in Europe. Many other expatriates headed there as well and my parents lived in a very diverse community, made up of both native Indians and expatriates.

Digging deep into their inner resources they found creative ways to survive. Papi realized he had useful skills as a manager and electrician, which he used in the villages and campamentos of the YPFB (Yacimientos Petroliferos Fiscales de Bolivia). Mami, who had never cooked in her life, cooked for the men. They moved around from place to place – from La Paz to Chulumani to Gran Chaco – whenever the work dried up and, as they recounted when I was a child, they were happy, despite living in basic one-room mud huts with vultures perched on the roof and a hole in the ground outside that served as toilet.

The time came when they were thinking of starting a family. Their life did not provide the necessary stability for children, though, and so they set their sights on Argentina.

Argentina prided itself on its neutrality. It turned into a favourite destination for Jewish refugees and, when it became clear how the war would turn out, for many Nazis and their families as well.

It is against this background that I tried to make sense of my childhood and upbringing, and how this experience shaped the woman I became.

2

My parents start
a new life

Buenos Aires, our new home, was a multi-cultural city which was divided into various communities – German, Spanish, British, and Italian, where I grew up.

My parents chose to live there mainly because it was cheap. Yet they bitterly resented being forced by life's circumstances to live amongst the "uncultured" working class'. What they minded most of all, however, was having to bring up their child there. To counteract any possible risk of contamination they forbade me to mix with the other children. When I begged to let me play with them, I was told they were a bad influence, ill-mannered, uneducated and generally uncivilized. In short, they were not people like "us" and my parents did not wish me to associate with them.

School was no better. The one they chose to send me to at great expense (instead of the local free school) was the Escuela Argentina General Belgrano, a German school which taught German and English. Their ambition was that I should become multilingual, which would open up all kinds of doors for me on the job market. The down side was that my fellow pupils, so they kept telling me, were children of either Jews or Nazis – neither of which it was safe to associate with or seen to be associating with.

As far as the Jewish children were concerned, my parents feared that being seen to associate with them might make me vulnerable in case of anti-Semitism, while they were also convinced that the beliefs of Nazi parents would have rubbed off on their children. In reality, and despite what they believed, there was never even the slightest hint of racism in school, neither from the teachers nor from the other pupils.

It is true that I was teased but only because I was the only girl, not only in that school but probably in the whole of Buenos Aires to have curly red hair and freckles. In fact, I never saw another redhead – child or adult – as long as I lived there.

I was also teased because of my surname Stroh, meaning straw. So the children would go into a sing-song: "she sunbathes with a strainer! She sunbathes with a strainer!" shrieking with laughter at their own wit or shouting that my head was filled with straw. Then they would run away – until next time. I never retaliated. I simply didn't know how. Witty retorts were way beyond me so I just stood there feeling embarrassed and helpless. When I told Papi he'd always come up with some clever one-liner to use next time, but I simply couldn't carry it off because they were his words, not mine and after trying a few times I never did again.

Not surprisingly, I used to feel lonely and isolated. The other children had formed cliques and the prettiest boys and girls were also the teachers' pets. I was at the bottom of the league.

My teacher was a spinster called Miss Berlin. She taught me throughout my school years and her approach never varied. To my parents she would say how smart I was, but in class she enjoyed humiliating me.

She would ask a question and then pick on a particular pupil. If the child didn't know the answer she enjoyed mocking them and encouraged the others to join in. I was one of her "favourites" in this ritual and this set the tone for the way the other children related to me.

One day a new pupil joined our class. I was 12 years old and she was 13. Gaby was a big-boned and ungainly teenager and she too became the focus of the other children's sarcastic comments. They teased her particularly cruelly about her clumsiness and large feet. She would blush furiously but, like me, she said nothing, merely keeping her eyes down and shuffling her feet. She also became an outcast and, as kindred spirits, we became friends and allies.

On one occasion, Miss Berlin decided to arrange a ballot to see who was the most popular pupil. Gaby had the bright idea that we vote for each other; that way, she said, we would each have at least one vote. It was small comfort, but not total humiliation, when it happened as she'd predicted.

I loved Gaby's company. She was curious about everything and very creative. She taught herself French and would go around reciting French verbs. She had just discovered 'The Three Musketeers' and would tell me all about the men's friendship and loyalty towards each other, their courage and their heroism.

She invited me one day to her home to play. "We're going to be the two musketeers", she announced. "You will be d'Artagnan and I will be Porthos". She then painted a huge black moustache on both of us, found some hats (probably her mother's) and taught me to fence with wooden sticks. When her mother called a halt to the proceedings for lunch we both fell about laughing and nearly choked on our sandwiches, watching each other's moustache move up and down as we chewed.

About a year later she forgot all about the French and turned her attention to Arabic culture teaching me some Arabic songs. She had seen a film about a Seikh and imagined romantic stories of being rescued by an Arab prince who would whisk her away from her humdrum life.

Her parents didn't know what to make of her and her mother would tell mine that she thought Gaby was a bit strange in the head. She then added "she takes after my ex-husband, you know".

Gaby never spoke much about her home life and coped by turning into herself, living out her fantasies and doing some writing. Not long after she turned 15 her family moved away and we lost touch. She was the only school friend I'd ever had.

When she left, there was a big hole in my life and still I was unable to make any new friends. Our "outsider" status had brought us together and, since there were no other "outsiders" at school, I reverted to my original status as an outcast. It is, therefore, not difficult to see how I came to be a self-conscious child, generally ill at ease in company, with no basic social skills and desperate to please.

The only contact I had was with my little neighbour, Olguita, but my parents disapproved of our friendship. They regarded her family as coarse and uncultured. Whenever I indulged in childish temper tantrums Papi would exclaim in horror to Mami, 'Look at how she dares to talk to me! She gets that from Olguita!" (who was roughly seven or eight years old, like me). "We should not allow them to associate or she'll get all her bad habits! Have you heard her insulting tone of voice when she addresses her own parents?!"

Papi would then turn to me and say, "if I'd been a friend and you talked to me like that you would have lost me by now – but I'm only your Papi". He would then insist I apologise and I'd be torn between feeling that it was unfair to be made to apologise when I knew I was "right" and not wanting to lose this pretend friend which clearly required me to suppress my emotions. Papi would use this imaginary friend a lot, the one I would lose if I had him or her in the first place, should I choose to continue to answer back or generally misbehave. I used to wonder if that was the reason I didn't have any friends.

This type of pressure created in me the belief that my way of being was bound to create a life of eternal loneliness and isolation.

When I was little, Papi always tried to prove his authority and credibility to me. There was one occasion which I remember very clearly because it shows he was never one to miss an opportunity to emphasize this authority in my childish eyes.

I was about six years old at the time and loud and stroppy. Outside a thunderstorm was raging. In the middle of my temper tantrum thunder cracked. I screamed. Papi turned to me and calmly said, "See? If you don't do as I say I will do that again." You never saw a child shut up so quickly.

Despite the fact that my parents loved me deeply I was an insecure child. They recognized my lack of self-confidence and would go to great lengths to reassure me how pretty and charming I was. Not only that, but very clever as well. And yet I still remember feeling, because of the many mixed messages I received, that I wasn't good enough.

These messages were not imagined. I remember they would say all these positive things to me and then at night, thinking I was asleep, I could hear them talking in worried tones about something I'd said or done that made no sense to them.

They particularly worried about whether or not I actually was smart. One thing Papi was wont to do was throw at me so-called "intelligence questions" designed to ascertain if I had any brains. Usually I failed. Whenever Papi snapped, "I have an intelligence question!" my stomach would churn and I would brace myself against getting it wrong yet again.

Here's one example:

Papi: "why does a man own a house with many rooms?"

Me (in a tentative tone of voice): "Because he wants to sleep each night in a different room?"

It would leave him literally tearing his hair out. At night they would discuss my various eccentricities, baffled. They even took me to a child psychologist who declared me to be not only fully mentally competent, but very bright indeed. My parents' reaction to her report was that she didn't know what she was talking about.

Ever since I can remember, there were two qualities my parents prized above all else: charm and being agreeable. They continually urged me to be both at all times in the deepest belief that my very survival depended on being liked. Yet whenever they pressed and prompted me to be charming I'd feel helpless and confused because I simply had no idea what being charming looked like. I wondered, how did I have to behave to be perceived as charming and agreeable? I simply didn't know.

My parents' expectations of me over the years felt oppressive. Their exhortations covered the whole gamut of phrases which they would utter without elaborating any further: "be a good friend", "be helpful", "be tolerant", "be liked", "be charming", "be ambitious", "don't be selfish", "don't try to be funny", "speak simply so you don't have nonsense coming out of your mouth", and, above all, "listen to us!"

Another popular refrain I was subjected to throughout my childhood was "don't be right, be successful". With hindsight I now realise that they meant I should not put my opinions across too forcefully, insist I was right or, worst of all, express anger and raise my voice.

However, I came to add further interpretations such as 'don't stand up for yourself', 'don't challenge or confront', 'give in', 'don't argue', and so on. To me 'be successful' meant 'be popular', 'be liked', 'be acceptable'. Consequently as an adult I was always tying myself into knots to be appealing to others, both personally and professionally, and seeing myself only through the eyes of others.

The grooming and coaching continued relentlessly. I remember once telling Papi that I 'wanted' something to which he replied, "young ladies don't say 'want'; they say 'would like'".

There were many instances, when I was made to feel "not OK". As a child I had boundless and unrestrained enthusiasm and would often run to Papi overflowing with excitement about something or other and the words would just tumble out of my mouth while he would tease me by saying "OK, go on, say it! 'the cow flew over the roof of the house!'" which I interpreted as "go on, say something stupid!". Even as an adult I could never bring myself to tell him how hurtful this was.

Good conversation was highly prized by Papi and he made friends with a couple of other families with whom they would occasionally exchange invitations for high tea and conversation. I was taken along regardless of whether there were children to play with.

Those who did have children encouraged us to make friends and would instruct us to go out and play which we did only reluctantly. We never did make friends, not even remotely, and we ended up avoiding each other wherever possible.

It is quite normal for parents to care about the safety and security of their children and my parents were no exception. Still, it doesn't explain their excessive over-protectiveness against disappointments of any kind, even with the most minor issues.

I remember playing a game of "figuritas" with my little friend, Olguita, seven at the time. It was a sort of 'head or tails' game with little cut-outs and the winner would take the "figuritas" from the loser. Olguita won regularly at this game of chance and, when I lost, I would start crying very loudly. Mami would rush in and make Olguita return the "figuritas" that she'd won fair and square.

It became second nature to avoid taking responsibility and my parents colluded. I most vividly recall, as a teenager, deciding to break off a relationship with a young man. I had hesitated for weeks and finally asked Papi to do it for me – which he did.

The belief that by following his advice at all times I would avoid disappointment was well meant, but even his greater life experience cannot take the place of your actually experiencing your own successes and inevitable disappointments. When I predictably fell flat on my face he would rub my nose in it with the refrain "I told you so!" and I became even more stubborn and resistant to his advice.

Papi had many of the basic crafts and skills needed to run a home – a bit of soldering, wiring, plumbing, carpentry – he could do it all. I loved to watch him, for example, unscrew plugs and do something mysterious that would restore a lamp to full working order.

As all responsible parents do, Papi warned me against touching plugs and sockets, but one day, when I was about seven years old, I failed to heed his advice with disastrous results. I was in my room reading when the lamp went out. Instead of feeling frustrated I was excited and decided I would sort it out just as I saw Papi do it.

I went to his toolbox and found a little screwdriver which I used to unscrew the little screws on the socket. It was all but seconds before I was struck with an electric shock that practically hurled me into the air. I yelped and started to wail loudly. Both my parents ran in to see what had happened. Mami hugged me and Papi said, "See, I told you not to touch anything! Will you now listen to me!" Chastened, I vowed never to touch anything electrical again; a vow I kept even when I married Jim to whom I was happy to defer all things electrical.

The experience taught me to be more cautious around sockets and plugs but didn't stop me from continuing to try and do other things which, again, didn't always turn out favourably. But, what upset Papi the most was my stubbornness in refusing to acknowledge his superior wisdom. The words he longed to hear from me were "You were right, Papi", words which rarely passed my lips and, when they did, only grudgingly.

This endless unconstructive criticism of my poor judgment made me fearful of trying out new things in case I messed up. I became someone who regarded mistakes as something to be feared and avoided at all costs or, if that was not possible, then concealed.

I also believed that I had to fit in with other people's view of how things "should be" in order to make myself 'acceptable'. Since I had no opinion of my own, I went along with this approach. However, none of it brought me the love and friendships I so craved. Praise and expressions of approval never seemed to really touch me, not even when they came from my parents because I never actually believed them. What

I really felt was a fraud and that they'd soon see through me, be totally put off by what they saw and walk away. I'd then be totally alone for ever. It became a picture I deeply believed.

This fear prompted me to try and be "all things to all people" but that didn't work either. People used to say "don't try so hard, just be yourself" but I had no idea what "being myself" was like. In fact, since I didn't know any differently, I believed I was "being myself" – whatever that meant.

What I didn't realise was that, in my efforts to be cheerful and chirpy I was actually relating the only way I knew how which was very limited, although I didn't realise it at the time.

I remember one day in my last year at school when I was 13 years old, a fellow pupil who recognised my sense of isolation tried to reach out to me by giving me some feedback about where I was going wrong, something which I was totally unable to handle. My response was to put my hands over my ears, turn away, and loudly go "la la la la! She shrugged and left the room.

On another occasion I had been saying some unkind things about a mutual acquaintance behind her back and she later confronted me. She was hurt and demanded an apology. In a chirpy, tone of pretend aggrieved innocence I replied, "I don't know what you're talking about but OK, I apologise if that's what you want". She turned, walked away and never spoke to me again.

When I was 12 and with the end of my primary education looming, Papi asked me what kind of work I wanted to do. I shrugged. He said, "In that case you are going to become a secretary." I replied, "OK, can I go out and play?" My future was sealed. I spent the next two years doing a secretarial course which constituted my secondary education.

3

My teenage years

My first job was as a typist. I was only 14 years old and Papi's earnest advice was, "keep your head down, do as you're told, and don't call attention to yourself."

Working as a typist was the first rung in a career that Papi had chosen for me. His reasoning was that my parents were all I had and their greatest nightmare was that something would happen to them and I would be left all alone, unable to fend for myself. It was Papi's belief that, whatever happened, as a secretary I would always be able to take care of myself. A plus point, as he saw it, was my facility with languages. I was fluent in Spanish and German, and was making relatively good progress with English – all of which, he believed, would make me a particularly attractive proposition to prospective employers. He even decided that, when the time came, I would go to evening classes to learn English shorthand and typing, which I did when I was 16 years old, all in preparation for the time when I would go to England, their dream for me.

As I grew into a young woman Papi would often comment how much like his sister Erika I looked. He would then tell me stories about her. Erika had actually died of cancer of the bone when she was in her early thirties but even as she lay in hospital, Papi told me, she had this amazing way with men and he would tell me about how they would fall all over themselves to ask her to marry them including, so he said, the surgeon himself.

I kept feeling I was a bitter disappointment to Papi because I was clearly so unlike her.

Papi would also prompt me about how I should behave with boys: he advised me to smile a lot and to never say or do anything that would betray the fact that I was smart – certainly not more than them because, he told me, "everybody knows that boys don't like smart girls." Therefore, if I didn't want to be left out I had to look at them adoringly and listen to them with rapt attention or look deeply into their eyes and say things like "You're so clever!" even if they didn't know their head from their arse.

Although I did try these techniques, I couldn't deliver them with assurance, nor follow them up with any degree of conviction. Eventually, even Papi had to admit that the clever seduction of boys/men was an absolute impossibility for me. Nor was flirting my thing. I lacked the confidence to carry it off. Nevertheless, he didn't give up.

When I was 18 I fell in love for the first time – with an older man. Lito Correa Lopez was 32, extremely handsome and, to me, the embodiment of sophistication. After an unhappy marriage he was now separated but, since divorce was not allowed in Argentina, he was, in the eyes of the Catholic Church, still married.

None of this mattered to me. I was totally smitten and he was attracted to me.

Unfortunately, Papi kept trying to orchestrate things from behind the scenes so it was no surprise that the relationship eventually foundered. The surprising thing was that when the end came I was not terribly distressed.

More than thirty years later, having at last started on this journey towards greater self-awareness to try and figure out why my life felt so empty and unfulfilled I came to realize just how deeply those early experiences had marked me.

And yet I have to admit that my mask did work for me.

4

I Journey to England
by Boat

The day had finally arrived. My parents had done their very best to prepare me for the next stage in my life and now they moved heaven and earth to obtain a one year work visa for England. They firmly believed that, professionally speaking, with this one year immersion, the sky would be the limit.

Standing on the boat waving goodbye I didn't, at first, feel sad. I was too excited. All around me so much to take in – fun, noise, music and excitement. Last-minute hugs and farewells, people crowding on the dock waving tearful goodbyes and blowing kisses, with lots of private sign language as well.

As the boat slowly started on its journey I only had eyes for my parents as they grew smaller and smaller in the distance. Gradually, people started to move away but I stayed on, still straining to see them. It was then, unexpectedly, that I saw my Papi cry. All the time he had been smiling and waving and letting me know how proud he was of me and then, thinking I was too far away to see, he turned to Mami and cried. It's a picture that's engraved on my heart forever.

I didn't stay sad for long. Leaving home for the first time in 1965 to travel to England at the ripe old age of twenty was incredibly exciting. The boat journey was everything I dreamed it would be. Above all, I was on my own for the first time and I felt free to do as I pleased, a thought that was both scary and exhilarating.

I had blossomed into a really attractive young woman and life looked like a whole lot of fun and promise. There were several people of my own age on the boat and just the fact that they were there instead of the constant diet of adult company felt incredibly liberating and enjoyable.

I no longer felt inhibited by Papi's constant exhortations to be one way or another.

5

I arrive in England

The boat docked in Southampton on a grey day on 13 July 1965. Arriving in England was a revelation to me and, without being able to explain why, I just knew I had "come home" even though I could hardly speak any English. That was probably because, for the first time in my life, I felt I could just be "me". I instantly fell in love with London and all these years later I love it still.

Those first impressions remain deeply engraved in my memory. Men with long hair, couples kissing in public, fashion photo shoots, film stars walking down London streets like anybody else. I didn't know where to look first.

For the first time I discovered just how kind and helpful people could be. Struggling with pounds, shillings and pence, there was always someone to help me and when I got lost, a kind person would generally accompany me since I had trouble understanding their directions.

To British eyes I looked foreign, probably even a little exotic: a pretty, freckly redhead with short, curly hair and dark brown eyes with (I was told) a charming accent. My halting English seemed to appeal and my Mediterranean disposition was perceived as colourful and unusual, particularly in those days when the average Londoner had limited exposure to foreigners. I was exuberant, loud and tactile which both attracted people and at the same time made them a little nervous.

Adjusting to British culture was not easy. In Argentina people stand fairly close to each other when talking, occasionally also touching. It didn't take me long to discover that this didn't go down very well in England. Whenever somebody felt I was standing too close to them they would discreetly step back and were uncomfortable if I touched them. Disconcerted, I couldn't understand what was wrong and thought the English distant and reserved.

I also found the men rather peculiar. They tended to project onto me fantasies from Hollywood films where Latin American women were portrayed as "exotic", somehow "wild" and "passionate" – whatever that meant – with a fiery temper. They would twist something I had just struggled to say and make it sound like a double-entendre, laughing uproariously at their own joke, a joke which I completely missed.

I remember feeling that people were not really seeing me but a figment of their own imagination. This created a lot of inner conflict: I went out of my way to present myself as an attractive foreigner even though I was not conscious of doing so but I didn't know how to handle people's perceptions of me and that made me feel somehow "odd". Even so, consciously or not, I always sought to put myself across in the way that would, I believed, maximise my appeal.

6

I Meet Jim

I first saw Jim on 30 October 1965 at a concert held at the German Institute in London. I showed up early and scanned the room to choose a seat. That's when I noticed him. I thought his hair was too long but I liked his looks. My first thought was if I got to know him, I would make sure he had his hair cut. I sat beside him – in an all but empty room, probably guaranteed to make him feel ill at ease although that had not been my intention – and engaged him in conversation.

Later he told me he thought my behaviour had been a bit odd but, since he couldn't get away from me without leaving the concert hall altogether, he had no choice but to respond to my efforts. In the course of the conversation I learned Shostakovitch was one of his favourite composers and that the following Saturday he was going to another concert dedicated exclusively to him. I had never heard of Shostakovitch but I decided to go too. I wanted to see Jim again even though he hadn't invited me along.

To my dismay, the turnout for Shostakovitch was so huge my hopes of seeing him again almost disappeared. My cheap seat was high up and I kept scanning the concert hall hoping to spot him, which I finally did, down in the stalls. I paid little attention to the music. All I was waiting for was the interval.

The minute the audience stopped clapping I raced down the stairs, then slowed down, walking casually towards him. I caught his eye and exclaimed with delight, "Mr Plumtree! What a coincidence!" Without waiting for his response I started gabbling about the music, the audience, the concert hall – anything that came into my head while he stood there looking bemused. As the interval bell rang I quickly suggested we meet up for a coffee afterwards and, to my relief, he agreed. I was elated. He barely stood a chance against my onslaught.

When it was all over Jim and I went to Lyons Corner House, around the corner. Sitting there all I knew was that I wanted to get to know him better. I found him very attractive: he had sexy dimples, beautiful hands, a lovely smile and kind eyes behind the spectacles. I really liked the sound of his voice. I wasn't too bothered that he wasn't particularly talkative – I talked enough for both of us. All he had to do was to sit there and let me get on with it, which he did very well.

My behaviour, especially at the outset, was influenced by the mask of my lack of authenticity – a socially acceptable mask, behaving in a way I imagined young women did when they were after a particular man. I flirted, flattered, gazed into his eyes and pretended to be fascinated by his every word – just the way I'd read about it in women's magazines and Papi had tried to teach me as a teenager. Papi said men loved being made to feel interesting and smart so, every once in a while I would murmur "Really? Tell me more" and when he faltered I would fill in the silence. All in all, I thought that first "date" went very well.

He suggested we meet again, so the following Sunday we went to London Zoo. Walking around I took hold of his hand and then he began to take the initiative.

When I first met him a whole range of factors came into play: partly it was my insecurity about my attractiveness and lovability, so I wanted to see if I could make him fall in love with me. But there was more to it than that. I was genuinely attracted to him, not only because I liked the look of him but also because he made me feel at ease, very different from the way I used to feel with Papi, compelled to perform in some way either by being witty, charming or a good conversationalist, preferably all three. With Jim I didn't feel I had to try hard at being anything other than what I was being at that particular time. That meant everything to me.

It was clear from the outset that he had no idea of how to deal with an attractive young woman who showed such blatant interest in him. He just went along with it. It was me who took the initiative in my obvious and clumsy way. I could see that Jim was inexperienced with women so I knew he didn't really stand a chance.

I soon discovered that not only had he never had any close relationships or romances, but he had also few casual friendships. The idea that he might have no need or desire for them never even crossed my mind. In fact, he was a loner and apparently content that way. Then I burst into his life and turned it upside down. Despite all the evidence to the contrary, I decided he had been waiting for the right woman and I was that.

He had a young German girl for a pen pal and occasionally met a gay man called Roy, also a loner. Then there was Lars, a Swede with whom he shared an interest in spectroscopy, the subject of Jim's thesis for his B.Sc. When Lars returned to Sweden, they corresponded regularly. Those were his only relationships.

I didn't mind his lack of friends. Nor did it strike me as particularly strange since I didn't have any close relationships either and my experience of romantic ones was fairly limited. I told myself, "I'm glad I don't have to share him with anybody else." My parents enjoyed nothing better than each other's company and I imagined it would be like that with us.

As I gradually began to understand what made him tick I learned that his slight deafness caused him to isolate himself and partly explained why he was a loner. He was also very comfortable in his own company.

He enjoyed solitary activities centred mainly around science, which became both his profession and his hobby, particularly computers in their infancy. He loved learning different computer languages and designing programmes. In his younger days he had enjoyed cycling across Europe. He had no interest in interacting with others at any but the most superficial level, regarding communicating with them hard work and stressful. By isolating himself he avoided anyone making demands or having expectations. Until I came into his life.

At first, although attracted to Jim, I didn't actually fall in love with him – not straight away. In the past I'd fall in love within a couple of days and out of love just as quickly. About four weeks after we first met he kept a date despite having a really bad cold. Although Jim did not look exactly alluring (eyes watering, red nose like Rudolph the reindeer's, coughing, sneezing and with a rough voice) my heart turned over with tenderness and I just wanted to look after him.

We cut that date short, I took him back to his digs and made him go to bed. I liked the idea of looking after him – I'd never done so before and he clearly enjoyed the novelty of it too. I was curious to see where he lived: a small room with a single bed and a wardrobe. Light came in from a tall and narrow window overlooking the back yard. The bathroom had to be shared with the other students and one ring was the sum of the cooking facilities.

He undressed while I turned my back to spare his (and my) blushes. Meanwhile, I occupied myself boiling water for tea and I even remember actually tucking him in. I stayed until he dozed off before tiptoeing out.

We met regularly after work while he was studying for his Bachelor of Science. Sometimes we'd go to see a play or a film or just have a bite to eat. He could never actually see me home because he lived in South Kensington and I in Barnet, and public transport stopped early in the evening.

Every once in a while I would go to his place so we could be alone together. Once, as we sat there cuddling he said to me, "Don't ever change." That's when I knew he really loved me. "I won't", I promised.

About four months into our relationship he said he had something really important to tell me. I looked at him expectantly.

"I'm slightly deaf", he confessed.

"I know", I replied, "what is it you want to tell me?"

He looked faintly annoyed. "I told you", he said, "I'm slightly deaf."

I burst out laughing. "I thought you were going to tell me something important!", I spluttered.

He looked as if I'd spoilt his big moment. When he recovered his composure he said, "I care about you, let's get married".

My reply was, "If you want a housewife then you've chosen the wrong woman because I'm not in the least domesticated, but if it's a friend you want then, yes." And we smiled at each other.

Jim wrote to my parents, to ask for my hand in marriage explaining that, for tax reasons, we had decided to marry in March (1966) just before the end of the current tax year. This change in marital status would entitle him to a tax refund which would come in handy as a deposit for a place of our own.

Two months later we were married. I'd only known him five months. The other reason for the rush was that my visa was only valid for one year and due to expire in three months time.

7

My life as a young bride

We started married life in a small, furnished ground floor flat in London's Clapham North. I was genuinely happy and deeply in love. I particularly loved the fact that Jim was physically affectionate. We would hold hands, cuddle and kiss, sometimes exchange a peck on the cheek. This was a completely new experience for me and I felt deeply nurtured and loved.

We continued going to concerts, the occasional play, the National Film Theatre on the South Bank and sometimes eating out. Slowly I realised that I much preferred concerts or plays, because sitting together over dinner highlighted how little we had to say to each other and a one-sided conversation was hard work.

When Jim and I married we were both virgins and totally inexperienced. While, on the one hand, my early experiences were mostly of discomfort and pain, on the other, I loved the closeness.

The one thing Jim was particularly good at was acting as "nurse" during my occasional periods of poor health; caring and patient, fetching and carrying for me, even though I was most ungrateful and impatient, frequently displaying my short temper and irritation at his "fussing".

But, as time passed, I longed for more. What I really wanted was for him to express his love by writing the occasional love note, waiting for me on my return from work, telling me how much he'd missed me. Or perhaps a surprise box of chocolates, a bunch of long stemmed red roses – something that would reveal his romantic side.

At first I used to write him love letters for no reason at all except that I did have a hidden agenda. I wanted to act out what, for me, romance looked like. Once I wrote him a particularly loving note saying how happy I was we'd found each other and were now together, as we were meant to be. I left it on the coffee table where I knew he would see it. I had an expectant half-smile on my face imagining how he would look and what he would say when he read it. He never mentioned it.

Eventually, when I couldn't wait any longer and asked him if he'd seen the note. "Yes, I did", he replied, "Don't do that anymore. It really doesn't do anything for me."

I felt crushed and deeply hurt and ran out of the room, crying. He didn't follow me and, for him, that was the end of the matter. He also made it absolutely clear from the very beginning that he didn't believe in celebrating Valentine's Day.

This hurt me all the more because it was in such complete contrast to how Papi expressed his love for Mami. Throughout their marriage he would leave her little love notes just to tell her how much she meant to him. Today, many of these slips are secured on a small notice board in my Mum's flat and, she tells me, not one day goes by without her reading them. She's over 90.

I suppose my fantasy was that Jim and I would have a similar kind of love, overtly expressed. Sadly, that expectation or fantasy never came about, however hard I tried to help make it happen.

It mattered to me that he would never say 'I love you' even when I asked him if he did, and when I said 'I love you' he'd simply smile and teasingly just said 'yes'. When I prompted him with 'Yes, and?' he'd say 'you love me'. Once when I asked him playfully "why do you love me?" he replied "because YOU love ME". I pouted and rolled my eyes in pretend amusement and a "you're so hopeless!" gesture, but deep down I felt hurt that he couldn't think of any particular quality in me that he found loveable.

I used to wonder if I was too needy so, after a while, decided that it wasn't really necessary for him to tell me 'I love you'; what was more important was for him to show his love through actions. But the loving actions I so longed for were few and far between. The gestures I craved were for the most part romantic, such as a spontaneous hug, but they would only come if I initiated them. Later, the love signs I longed for became more practical. For example, I worked full time and came home tired from the working day and commute, with dinner still to prepare. Jim, on the other hand, was at home all day working on his thesis and, although I realise he was busy, at least he didn't have to travel. I would have felt appreciated, as well as relieved, if he'd helped around the house by at least clearing up – but he didn't.

Unfortunately, when he asked me to marry him and I told him that I was undomesticated I had told him the absolute truth. I absolutely detested housework. Jim didn't care about the state of the flat and, since he was unwilling to help out, I decided that I didn't either. I justified it to myself thinking, if I didn't spend time doing housework neither of us cared about, then we could spend more time together. It became a way to bury my hurt and resentment about feeling unsupported.

I imagined most couples had some common goal, either raising a family or pursuing a shared interest. I yearned to share with him the things that mattered to me, but he was unresponsive. And although I wanted to support him I found it impossible to do this because he didn't feel the need to share anything with me.

Over the years I worked hard at showing him how much I loved him. Cooking special meals and experimenting was something we both enjoyed. I was thrilled to find a common interest and collected a huge library of cookbooks. Jim even joined me in my shopping expeditions to the supermarket.

At first his approval of my efforts was satisfying but his response didn't address what I truly wanted and, eventually, the novelty wore off. In the end, it didn't bring me the intimacy I craved.

Jim did not fit in with my fantasies of the "ideal" man. When all my efforts to show how much I loved him failed to elicit any response I became depressed. I felt ignored and of no importance to him.

However, I rarely allowed myself to remain hopeless for long. Instead I developed techniques and distractions to help me snap out of it. I pretended things weren't so bad, that it didn't really matter, I didn't really mind, others had much worse experiences. I concentrated on keeping busy. It never took long for my fantasy of "happy marriages" to return.

Jim developed a deeply hurtful habit that told me that I embarrassed him. Whenever I became upset or raised my voice in front of other people he would apologise saying "she's Argentinian, you know" – as if that explained everything. Although feeling dismissed as overly emotional, true to form, I didn't say anything.

I decided to try managing our finances, a first for me, but I like taking on new challenges.

Initially I found it difficult to live within our means. Jim was still studying and, although I was working full time, my earnings were around "minus average" and we were spending more than I earned. I said nothing to Jim because I enjoyed going out and was sure that, if he knew, he would cut down on entertainment. I was not prepared to do that.

Our finances were not the only subject I kept to myself. Since he didn't respond when I told him about my worries I thought he would love me more if I were cheerful and upbeat. Anxieties about my job or times when I felt sad or worried were kept secret.

But when evening came and we sat on the settee, cuddling, all I could feel was his love and tenderness as he held me while we were watching the telly, a favourite activity for both of us.

His tenderness was so important to me and over the years, when I felt hurt or disappointed at something he had said or done – or, more likely, something he had not said or done – I would comfort myself that he loved me really and the proof was that he would put his arm around me.

8

I learn to suppress
my feelings

We had been married some 18 months. I hadn't yet learned that it was useless to have a row with Jim because he simply withdrew within himself and refused to respond or react in any way. I remember one particular occasion. Something he'd said triggered intense frustration in me and I started shouting. He kept ignoring me and, the more he did, the louder I shouted until, finally overcome with rage, I grabbed him by the shoulders, shaking him so hard that his head bobbed backwards and forwards and accidentally hit against the wall. The red fog of rage that had enveloped me lifted and I was appalled, not only at my actual violence but also the potential for violence that I felt within me. In fact, I was so distressed that I decided never ever to express rage again, neither towards him nor anybody else.

Having made that decision I suppressed all feelings of anger, without realising that it continued to simmer away below the surface. I may not have noticed, but others did, however hard I tried to pretend that everything was sweetness and light between us.

Esther, a friend of mine, came to visit one day. Jim and I didn't have any mutual friends, so he usually kept out of the way. Left alone we felt free to talk openly.

I had had a row with Jim shortly before she arrived. Actually, 'having a row' implies a quarrel with both of us joining in. In fact, Jim and I never had rows. It was always one-sided so, as all my past experiences of "non-rows" I was left feeling resentful, angry and frustrated. But, as Esther was there, I tried to push my feelings aside. Jim pottered around oblivious to our desire for privacy and I felt the anger rising. True to form, I expressed only mild impatience, saying in what I believed was a light-hearted tone of voice, "Darling, Esther and I need some time on our own so we can tell dirty jokes without being overheard". I thought I was being really clever. However, as soon as Jim walked out of the room, Esther turned to me and said, "You know, I felt really uncomfortable just then. Did you notice you were smiling at him through gritted teeth? Even I could tell you only just stopped yourself from hitting him." I felt exposed but made light of it. "And I thought I hid it so well", I joked feebly. We changed the subject and nothing more was said.

Desperate to cling to the façade of "happy marriages" I used all kinds of self-deception, pretending I didn't really mind; that I didn't really feel hurt; "it" wasn't such a big deal and I was making too much of "it"; in any case, I could handle "it". For the most part I really believed my fantasy of being loved. As banal as it may sound, there's none so blind as he who does not want to see.

Actually, my pretences weren't all that hard to keep up. I had been groomed from childhood and, by then, I didn't even realise I was pretending.

9

We embark on a
new life

For the first few months of our marriage I helped Jim by typing up his thesis. We hired an electric typewriter and every evening I spent an hour or so after dinner working on it. Happy to support him, I felt I was making an important contribution.

Jim graduated at a time when the economy was going downhill and he had a hard time finding a job. That's when the Americans stepped in. American scientific research organisations came to England in droves offering good opportunities. It was a time known as "the great brain drain" and Jim was one of many scientists they snapped up. Several companies expressed interest and he was invited to the States where he spent several weeks doing a round of job interviews. We kept in close touch, mostly by letter or telegrams. I missed him terribly. Sometimes we managed to talk on the phone but lines were very crackly so the conversations were unsatisfactory.

Then a telegram came. He had been offered a position with Sprague Electric in Nashua, New Hampshire. Our lives were about to change hugely.

10

We move to the USA

We left England in early December 1966 and travelled by boat to Buenos Aires to visit my parents. I was thrilled to show Jim off to them and they took him into their hearts straight away. Jim was taken aback. After a solitary life he was thrust into the arms of a highly demonstrative and affectionate family.

Jim's own experience of a family could not have been more different. His Dad had died of tuberculosis just before he was born and his Mum brought him up single-handedly, working hard to survive. Jim didn't talk too much about her. When I pressed him he said she worked in a tobacconist shop beside a railway line and, from what I gathered, she wasn't particularly physically affectionate. She remarried shortly after the war. Her second husband, Harold, was also fairly laconic and unsociable. However, despite neither of them being overly demonstrative they had a good marriage. Then one day, when Jim was 16, he came home to find his Mum lying on the carpet, having died from a blood clot. My heart went out to him for what I imagined had been a deeply traumatic experience, but Jim never mentioned it again.

After her death he and Harold lived together. Both were totally undomesticated and easy-going and the arrangement worked well until he married a widow, who made it clear she didn't want Jim around. So he moved into the University's student accommodation.

So, when my parents hugged him to their bosom, both literally and figuratively, he didn't know how to respond. He did come to love them in his own way, but was never demonstrative nor did they get close to him no matter how hard they tried. Papi, in particular, hoped for heart-to-heart conversations with his "son" and the occasional phone call but that didn't happen unless I specifically called Jim to the phone on special occasions. I know they found it disappointing although they eventually got used to it. My belief is that they expected too much of him.

Our stay was a huge success. Mami, a terrific cook, treated us to wonderful meals and the highlight of our stay was a surprise week's holiday at the seaside resort of Mar del Plata.

We left the warmth and sun of Buenos Aires landing in New York on 1 January 1968, a bitterly cold grey day. We were both shell-shocked by the sudden change in climate. The city felt intensely aggressive and we were well and truly out of our depth. We only stayed a couple of days because our final destination was a small town in New Hampshire called Nashua. It only had 30,000 inhabitants. We flew to Manchester airport where we were welcomed by Barry, Jim's immediate manager and his wife, SallyAnn. They were both warm and friendly but I felt physically and emotionally drained from the journey, and found it difficult to respond with the same heartiness. Jim was glued to the car window. Exploring new places was something he'd always enjoyed and, to the amusement of both Barry and SallyAnn, he kept up a running commentary. I was tired and felt overloaded with all the new sights and sounds – just too much to take in.

They had temporarily arranged for us to stay at a local motel, the Berkshire Country Inn which looked incredibly luxurious. They also urged us to learn to drive and buy a car.

Those first few days whilst sorting out a car and driving lessons we used to go for walks which caused a stir amongst the drivers because, as we soon learned, in the States nobody walked anywhere.

It was while we were walking along a snow drift that Jim slipped on the ice and broke his right wrist. After the panic was over and he had his arm in a cast we had to review our plans. Being right-handed, he was not able to fend well for himself and that meant I had to learn to drive first so that I could be his chauffeur for the next several weeks.

I was right about my impression of the Berkshire Country Inn. It was indeed luxurious and, as we found out soon enough, with prices to match. It became even more urgent that I learn to drive because we needed wheels to be able to find a place to rent.

One of the problems with a different currency was that I couldn't really get a handle on what we were spending. I also discovered that while in England it was generally accepted that people should try to live within their means, something I often failed to do, in America thrift was actively discouraged. It was essential we incur debt via hire purchase in order to establish an identity. Without debt, we didn't exist. With a home to furnish and a car to buy I was more than happy to oblige and Jim went happily along with it.

Even with his arm in a cast Jim's enjoyment and enthusiasm for our new life was undiminished and he was busy with his new job. I had a very hard time, though, fitting in with American culture.

Initially, I was fully occupied trying to find a place to live and I did eventually find an apartment which was absolutely fabulous. I had never before seen a kitchen so luxuriously appointed; it even included a dishwasher which clinched it for me. The rent was very high but I had fallen in love with the place. Jim tried to resist pointing out that it would put a real burden on our finances, but I was determined to have it and promised we would be able to handle it by cutting costs elsewhere. Determined to get my way, I would have promised anything.

In the beginning, SallyAnn and the wives of Jim's colleagues invited me to their coffee mornings. As a rule, the wives of senior management did not work. I politely refused all their overtures until eventually they gave up. Going to church was another way of socialising in Nashua, we were told. Since Jim never went to church, it was he who declined this time. The idea of making small talk filled me with horror so, when they stopped approaching us I felt relieved. Making an effort to be part of a group where I felt an outsider harked back to Papi's demands and expectations of me to be charming, agreeable and sociable. I was more interested in finding a job and, with my secretarial skills, there was plenty of choice. The problem was not finding a job but keeping it, because in the beginning, I simply couldn't understand the American accent well enough to take shorthand or use the Dictaphone.

After being fired yet again I sank into a depression, turned to food for comfort and spent most of my days in bed. Over the next three months I put on over four stone in weight.

Jim had no idea how to deal with me. His comments about my weight provoked me into eating all the more and he was often impatient and irritated. My life finally improved when one of the employment agencies threatened to drop me from their books if I refused any more interviews. That proved to be a turning point because the very next job I went for turned out to be the one I loved the most.

Around that time we had an even greater worry. We were notified by the US Government that Jim was liable to be called up and sent to Vietnam. At first we thought the letter was a huge joke or some administrative error, but it was neither. When it eventually sank in that they were serious we became absolutely terrified. Jim went to see Barry, his manager, and said that at no point in the interview process had he been warned that he might be called up. Barry made a lot of reassuring noises and promised to write to the State Department to say that Jim was carrying out essential work, but it made no difference. In the end, what saved him was that he failed his physical because of his poor hearing and, worse from the Army's point of view, he was also colour blind. When the letter finally came we were both hugely relieved.

Life in Nashua was as different from London as is possible to imagine. After six months we decided to buy a home of our own. That involved buying land first, then employing an architect and having our home built.

Jim and I would visit the building site – our future home – on a regular basis taking masses of photographs at every stage of development. The land was surrounded by lots of trees and the back overlooked a tiny forest of pine trees. What we hadn't realised was that ours was the first plot of many to be sold and we ended up surrounded on all sides except the back by similar looking homes, built so closely that we could almost look inside each other's windows.

Nevertheless, we were happy there. I spent a lot of time, energy and money furnishing our new home, a project which took me the best part of a year to complete. Once that was done I was faced yet again with a yawning emptiness and lack of purpose in my life.

I wondered if this wasn't the right time to think about having children. When Jim and I first got together we very briefly touched on the subject. He liked the idea, but I knew I wasn't ready so we agreed that I'd go on the Pill for a couple of years.

More than two years had passed and I felt that perhaps it was time to stop the Pill and try to get pregnant. As it turned out, getting pregnant wasn't happening so we both underwent a variety of tests all of which proved that nothing stood in our way to parenthood. We were advised to be patient. Then, something unforeseen happened that alerted me to my true feelings about parenthood. After about two years with Sprague Electric Jim was made redundant. To me, this was not unexpected. I had tried to warn Jim and persuade him to look for another job while he was still working, but he wouldn't listen. He knew things had become difficult for the company but felt strongly that he owed them his loyalty. Sadly, it was not reciprocated.

However, what struck me was my relief at his redundancy. "Thank God", I thought, "now I can go back on the Pill." I was shocked by the unexpectedness of this thought. Jim's redundancy gave me the perfect excuse.

It was in such times of crisis that I really came into my own. My first challenge was to economise and I became highly creative at making tasty dishes with leftovers. I asked my manager for all the overtime going and even gave up my fifteen days holiday entitlement in return for the pay.

I also put in a lot of effort to remain cheerful in order to prop Jim up. His job searching efforts can best be described as listless which caused me intense frustration and resentment. My way of dealing with the situation was to take over this area as well. I'd go to the local library and scan the job ads, then draft the letter of application which I got Jim to write. I even put together his CV. The only thing I couldn't do was to go to the actual job interview in his place, which caused me a lot of anxiety being the one thing I couldn't control.

I had turned into my parents. They always knew what was right for me and kept wanting me to do things their way. And now, here I was, doing the same to Jim.

Times were grim. Fortunately, the Americans provided social security which helped us survive. However, after a few months of what we regarded as intense deprivation and with the risk of both of us sliding into depression we decided to take drastic action: we blew a whole week's unemployment benefit on a long weekend in New York. We returned totally skint and fully re-energised.

Jim did eventually find another job but that one, too, ended in redundancy after less than a year. Scientists and managers across the whole of the scientific research industry based in Massachussetts were now affected. This became known as "the great crash of Route 128" and affected Joe, my own manager and myself.

Not everybody regarded being made redundant as a catastrophe however. Many saw it as an opportunity to follow their heart and so it was not an uncommon sight to see scientists becoming taxi drivers, going into the construction industry or real estate, as did Joe, my ex-manager and his wife, Louise.

For us, though, it was the last straw and we decided to sell our house and return home. So, after three years we returned to England, arriving on a grey and bitterly cold day in January 1971. We had only been married five years.

11

My mask doesn't work

Once back in England, survival became our common purpose. Since all our riches were tied up in our house in the States we were temporarily broke until it was sold which did not take long. Unfortunately, though, we found ourselves in the middle of a bitter Post Office strike that lasted nearly two months which delayed the receipt of monies from the sale.

While all this was going on surviving on a day-to-day basis became a real challenge. Eating became a luxury and we used to make bets as to who would spend less on food that day. On one occasion I actually won – I'd spent 3 old pennies on a hamburger in Wimpy's against his 4.

Having to tighten our belts, metaphorically speaking, and walking everywhere now that we no longer had a car meant that I was also able to tighten my belt in a physical sense because the weight I had put on in Nashua began to literally fall off me.

Hunger and living in seedy rooms drove us both to frantic job searching efforts until finally, after almost a year of struggling and only the occasional secretarial temping or short-term job, we both found permanent jobs, starting on the same day in Welwyn Garden City, Hertfordshire: 1 November 1971 – Jim as a researcher with Rank Xerox and me as a secretary with Smith Kline & French.

Although it had not been my own choice to become a secretary, I did actually enjoy most of the jobs I'd held as long as I had a good relationship with my manager and colleagues, which I usually did.

I was still ill at ease around new people but fortunately a colleague, Janet, took me under her wing and, before I knew it, she had introduced me to all her friends who welcomed me warmly. For the first time I belonged to a social circle, a real group of friends. Janet was the driving force, organising all kinds of events – afternoons at the local swimming pool, a couple of Kenwood open-air concerts, and visits to each other's houses. However, the most important and involving activity was the local amateur dramatics society where my accent was both a bonus and a major limitation – I loved it all.

A rediscovered passion for cooking gave me the confidence to invite my new friends over for a meal, something I loved. They also enjoyed those occasions and would often tell me how much they looked forward to them.

Jim did not feel at ease around company. He once told me that his hearing caused him difficulties picking out the various strands of a conversation. I realised that, at dinner parties, people had to fight for "air time" and Jim was not good at it. I felt very protective of him and made sure he got his chance when he wanted to make a contribution.

I became very popular because people liked my sunny disposition. I had always fostered a bubbly and happy persona to the point where people would comment approvingly: "You're always so cheerful!" At one level this certainly worked for me.

Di, a work colleague, and by no means the only one, would often come over to my desk and say "I thought I'd come over for you to cheer me up." And I would put on my smile and my solicitous face and pour good cheer all over her. Then she'd say "Thanks" and walk away. She never asked me how I was feeling nor did anybody else. They didn't need to ask; they "knew". I was feeling cheerful. The idea that I might not feel in the slightest bit cheerful never crossed anybody's mind and, to be fair, I deliberately hid any un-cheerful feelings I might have had because I believed they would put people off. More than that, I had a strategy in place which involved being as supportive as I knew how, cheerful, undemanding, loyal and fun to be with.

There was a saying around at the time which was, in fact, part of a poem by Ella Wheeler Wilcox. I haven't heard it for a long time, but it made a deep impact on me then. The part of the poem which so affected me goes: "Laugh and the world laughs with you; cry and you cry alone" and continues "...for the grand old earth/must borrow its mirth/but has sorrows enough of its own."

Certainly the first part of this poem fitted perfectly with my beliefs about how I should be in order to be loved. I interpreted any other way of being as needy and demanding, something I would never permit myself.

I also never experienced any conflict since I'd go to any lengths to side-step it. Conflict scared me. I genuinely believed that it signified the end of a relationship and I certainly could not allow that to happen. To that end I made sure I never provoked anyone or put myself in a situation where I would have to confront conflict. Some of these approaches were quite simple, for example, I tended to assume that friends would forget we'd arranged to meet so I made sure they didn't by ringing them up to remind them. In the normal course of events there was nothing unusual about this, except my underlying belief that, if they were to forget I'd have to get angry – and I couldn't take the risk.

More serious were my efforts to swallow disappointments and hurts telling myself that they didn't really matter. It wasn't that I was afraid to say something; I was afraid of what they might say in return. What if I couldn't handle it? What if they shouted back at me or said something really hurtful? And if they walked away from me? I really believed that would be the end of the world. I couldn't imagine anything worse.

Meanwhile, at home, my love life wasn't working particularly well. Jim's Circadian rhythm and mine kept sabotaging us. I was a lark while Jim was an owl. He would come to bed at about 1:00 in the morning feeling frisky while I was due to get up early to go to work. Although he too had to go to work, he could easily manage with only 4 or 5 hours sleep whereas, if I slept 7 hours or less I would be a total wreck the following morning. I pretended to be fast asleep until, eventually, he would give up. There was another reason too, one that I wouldn't admit to myself. Our love-making didn't feel loving, tender or intimate. I continued to take the initiative because I yearned for the closeness but, when we made love, I ended up wishing I hadn't bothered.

Again, my mask proved to be a great ally in my battle against truth and reality both at home and at work – and my mask always worked – or so I believed.

I remember one particular occasion. The offices were open plan but managers were allowed screens for quasi-privacy. I was in my manager's cubicle by myself, sorting some papers. It was close to lunch time.

Without any warning I suddenly burst into silent sobs. There appeared to be no trigger or at least none that I was aware of. After a few interminable minutes I decided it was time to pull myself together and said to myself, "OK, it's time to put my cheerful mask on again". I was shocked to the core at this thought since I hadn't realised that I was actually wearing a 'cheerful mask'. However, this thought disappeared from my consciousness as quickly as it had surfaced. The strain of projecting an unremittingly cheerful persona, despite feeling disappointed and unhappy in my marriage, finally was taking its toll.

I slid into depression for which the doctor prescribed Valium. Valium was the miracle drug at the time and, in my case, the prescription was ready the minute I walked into his surgery. I actually welcomed the Valium. All I had to do was ask.

I discovered that it helped me take the edge off the worst of the pain of feeling lonely and isolated, empty and disconnected which I overlaid with this mask of always being cheerful. Although the numbing worked relatively well I still suffered from bouts of intense weeping, which I did in secret so nobody would know.

Nobody knew I was depressed and taking antidepressants, not even Jim. I carried on my job as usual, on automatic pilot and with my cheerful mask firmly in place although I was churning inside. I felt I had no-one to talk to even though I don't think this was, strictly speaking, true. There were people in my life who would have listened but three things held me back.

One reason was that I judged my feeling of sadness and hopelessness to be excessive. The second, which flowed from the first, was that it therefore followed no-one else could handle them except me, the hero. Thirdly, I couldn't allow myself to admit to feelings which did not fit my self-image or were concealed behind my Mask.

The doctor to whom I turned had either very little time or very little interest. The Valium, which I wanted to help me numb my pain, ended up numbing all my feelings.

At work people kept asking me when Jim and I were going to have children. At first, I would brush the questions aside with some kind of flip remark but they became increasingly insistent. I decided to deal with the question honestly and replied that I didn't really want children. The hostility this generated took me completely by surprise. One man actually spat at me "You castrating bitch!" Later I found out that he and his wife had unsuccessfully been trying to have a baby for years.

Seriously pressured, the best way to stop this business in its track was to say, with a sad expression on my face, that Jim and I couldn't have children. Everyone backed off and gave me the breathing space I craved.

I needed to do something to push away my unhappy thoughts and I began to spend more and more money as a means of distracting myself from my depression. I soon discovered that having money to spend was fun, and I always had money with a credit card. Since I would also only re-pay a little more than the absolute minimum every month I never felt in the slightest bit deprived. I usually did little more than briefly cast my eye over the monthly credit card statements and ignored the ever-increasing debt.

I loved nice clothes and particularly enjoyed going on regular spending sprees. People always complimented me on my appearance and clothes, and I'd go to great lengths to ensure that my clothes were classy (by which read 'expensive') and the cut and colour combinations reinforced my self-image of a confident, friendly, approachable, informal yet professional woman. I put a lot of thought, effort and money into promoting that image and, judging from people's comments, it clearly worked.

When it came to going out with friends I used to say, jokingly, that I enjoyed "good food, good wine and good company – though not necessarily in that order" although that was exactly the order in which I enjoyed them. I would always suggest fairly expensive restaurants which I tended to call "treats". The point of choosing these restaurants had only partly to do with the quality of the cooking; mostly, it was to show I was just as successful, as I believed my friends to be. I believed that they had money to burn and I'd rather have died than admit there was something I couldn't afford. Taking taxis home after work was another treat I would indulge in several times a week to save waiting at the bus stop, particularly in winter when it was cold and dark.

All these treats created the self-image of a confident, successful, attractive and fun person to be with – and my Mask supported me in this endeavour.

I continued taking the Valium. It was as if I was a character on stage, playing a part (my False Self), while the Valium suppressed my genuine Self, the one in pain.

Meanwhile, my parents and I finally recognised how much we missed each other and decided that, after almost eight years, it was time for a visit. This finally came about in May 1974.

Having rained for months without let up, the weather suddenly cleared and the whole of that May was radiantly sunny. Then, as soon as my parents left, the weather broke again and it rained for pretty much the rest of the year.

But, during those sun-filled days, we had a wonderful time together. That was when Jim was at his best, planning where we would go and reflecting on what we might all enjoy, and my parents – and I – appreciated both his efforts and all the places we visited.

Apart from the obvious tourist spots, we spent a long weekend in Bath, went to the theatre and cinema and spent lots and lots of time just being together.

I put a lot of effort into planning special meals for them. Spurred on by Mum's great reputation as a hostess, I set out to impress with my recently acquired, excellent cooking skills. I was a great success. I also invited my friends around for a meal to meet my parents.

By the time my parents left I had put on 14 pounds – in just one month.

I was overwhelmed with a whole host of feelings, the strongest of which was loneliness. Deep down I had known all along how desperately lonely I felt, even before my parents' visit. But I pushed it way down inside me because I didn't know what to do about it. My parents reignited a feeling of love, caring and companionship that I had forgotten and not experienced in my marriage so, once they had gone, it was like an unwelcome truth pushing itself into my consciousness.

However, instead of confronting the truth of the emptiness and isolation within my marriage, I went on a diet. I could do something about my weight even if I didn't know what to do about the rest of my life.

I refocused all my energies on my weight and felt anxious, depressed and angry at myself for having let it go this far – my weight, that is, not my life.

A few days after I started my diet I noticed that this time it was different. I was not plagued with the usual hunger pangs nor the normal resentfulness and irritability. I was delighted. It had never been this easy and the weight was literally dropping off me.

This lasted for around six or seven weeks. Then disaster struck, at least that was how I interpreted it. I started feeling hungry again. I really panicked, terrified that I would become huge and grotesque.

Then I had a really exciting idea. No need to be afraid of eating or ballooning. As the idea gradually took shape I felt an intense sense of power. I could eat whatever I wanted, as much as I wanted, whenever I wanted – all I had to do was to make myself vomit afterwards. Now I would finally have total control over my body – even if I had no control over any other area in my life.

Nobody noticed, least of all Jim. He saw me eating huge amounts but didn't notice that I was, at the same time, losing a lot of weight.

It was Doug, a colleague at work, who first commented on it. No. That's not strictly speaking true. Others, women, had commented that I was getting too thin but I took it that they were just jealous. But with Doug it was different not only because, as a man I didn't sense any jealousy from him, but also because we were mates and I knew he cared about my welfare. So, when he suggested I went to see the doctor I took him seriously.

The doctor was very patient with me. It took persistent questioning before I finally admitted I was making myself sick. He asked me how I did it and I held up my finger. I looked at his face as I told him and his expression caused a deep knot of anxiety in my stomach.

"What you're suffering from", he told me, "is an eating disorder called bulimia. If we don't do something about this immediately it could have potentially fatal consequences. The first thing we're going to do is arrange an appointment with a psychotherapist."

As I sat there I realised I had always suspected deep down that there was something seriously wrong with me and it was a relief that somebody else finally knew and was taking steps to help me. My burden was about to be shared.

I still hadn't told Jim what was happening and only did so after several sessions with the psychotherapist.

Whenever I had eaten something and was going through this intense struggle, with the psychotherapist's support, of trying not to make myself vomit, Jim's way of supporting me was along the lines of "pull yourself together" and "don't be silly".

The process was incredibly hard because I was overwhelmed with terror that, if I stopped making myself sick, I would grow hugely fat. That was driven by the strong belief that, by stopping myself from vomiting, I was actually betraying myself.

My fear was that if I couldn't at least have this "tool" then there was nothing left. Except that I didn't really know what I meant by 'nothing'. All I knew was that I felt this sense of dread I couldn't put a name to. I just felt it was somehow connected with my bulimia.

I realised that Jim was incapable of giving me genuine support – I had to face this crisis on my own.

The psychotherapist helped, but progress seemed slow as she concentrated mostly on control issues which I persistently denied, rather than on the immediate crisis which was my fear of eating.

I was not quite as much on my own as I had thought though. Throughout this crisis I continued with my job as secretary to the Sales Manager, Wayne Woodrow. Over the years I had been working for him we had developed a good relationship and, occasionally, I would confide in him. This was one such time. One day I got a phone call at the office from his wife, Sandi. She had heard about what I was going through and was very sympathetic and supportive. With infinite patience she showed me how to gradually start eating again – one grape or one tiny piece of cheese at a time and then gradually increasing the amounts, bit by bit. I certainly needed her care and she was there to give it to me.

The lack of proper nutrition over much of the year had taken its toll. My energy levels were low and doing anything required a lot of effort.

One day in early 1975 while I was still undergoing treatment, Jim and I attended a performance of 'The Voodoo Dances of Brazil' at the Round House in London.

As usual, we had the cheap seats at the back but that didn't matter. The rhythm mesmerised me partly because of their own beauty and partly because South and Latin American music had been part of my childhood. As the performance neared the end, the dancers invited members of the audience to come on stage. Without realising how I got there, I found myself on stage dancing joyfully alongside them. I felt as if the music had got deep into my body and my soul. That was the turning point and beginning of my recovery.

Life went back to "normal", meaning that I started eating healthily again and gradually felt physically and emotionally stronger. I was beginning to feel more settled but this stage didn't last long.

12

How I managed change

After nearly five years in the same job I was restless. Acting in a support role to someone else, which I had always enjoyed, was now losing its appeal. I considered what it could be like to take centre stage and have accomplishments of my own. There were many articles in women's magazines offering a myriad of ideas, including the possibility of returning to full-time education. They were interesting but, I told myself, that's all they were, articles.

Meanwhile, Jim had troubles of his own, feeling deeply unhappy in his job. By inclination and training he was both a scientist and a researcher, but his job demanded that he be forceful and sociable, work with the team and put his views across in a confident and articulate way. In their efforts to support him, the company sent him to an assertiveness training course which he loathed. The next step up the corporate ladder was to a managerial position which he resisted. This caused a bottleneck, because people in positions junior to him could not be promoted. Then, almost miraculously, an internal post came up that appeared to suit him perfectly. Unfortunately, it was far from Ware – in Gloucester, to be precise.

Gloucester was a pleasant enough city but, as far as I was concerned, in the middle of nowhere, four hours from London. It represented everything I didn't want – having to give up my home, my job and my friends.

We had a very nice house in Ware, Hertfordshire, an easy commute to both our work places in Welwyn Garden City and the occasional day out in London.

Both my parents – but Papi, in particular – had fixed ideas about what "success" looked like and our lifestyle was it: good jobs with prestigious companies and a lovely home near London. What else could a proud parent wish for? They loved to talk about their "children" to their friends back in Buenos Aires and boast about how their daughter was a successful PA with Smith Kline & French and her husband, a highly-regarded scientist with Rank Xerox. They were genuinely, intensely proud of our achievements.

I supported Jim fully in submitting his job application (because, my Mask insisted, that's what "good" wives do) but I never for a second believed he would be offered the position. When he was, I was totally devastated. I would lose everything I cherished most. Meanwhile I also ignored the changes simmering inside me and in my own working environment.

Wayne, my manager, had returned to Canada and I didn't hit it off nearly as well with his replacement. Some of my friends were also leaving. Everything that had attracted me to my job was in a state of flux. Yet, although I no longer enjoyed it as much, I continued to cling on.

These then were the struggles I was experiencing when my parents waded in with their typical "I know what's best for you" approach.

While I had my own issues to battle with, my parents were pressurising us to stay put. It was the prestige of a beautiful house near London versus the Cotswolds "in the middle of nowhere" – my very words.

The pressure from my parents, especially Papi, tore me apart, but I didn't tell them.

I felt selfish that my own needs conflicted with Jim's. My Mask's insistence that, as a warm-hearted and generous woman I had to set my own needs and desires aside made me resentful. Why was it always me who gave up my way of life to follow Jim wherever his job took him? I hadn't minded moving to the States, because I hadn't been in London long enough to make friends and settle down. But now it was very different; now it did matter.

Jim was so excited about the new job he hardly noticed my distinct lack of enthusiasm and, in any case, knowing how he felt about the current job, I felt unable to insist we stay. With all this going on inside and the conflict with my parents increasingly fraught, I became really stressed.

Our letters always seemed to be at cross purposes, because I couldn't tell them or anybody else how I really felt. Trapped.

Like my parents, I too wanted us to stay in Ware but was powerless to resist. It was a lose-lose situation: agreeing with my parents felt disloyal while disagreeing with them was confrontational.

I wanted to shout at them "Leave me alone! Stop interfering!" but, of course, I didn't. Instead, I pretended that certain particularly tricky letters had not arrived. My parents knew I was lying and that added to the bitterness of the conflict. I had no-one to turn to and my belief that I could protect others from pain and was strong enough to handle the situation was falling apart. I wanted to run away and eventually I did, metaphorically speaking – again with the help of Valium which numbed the worst of my inner conflicts and helped me function to some extent.

In the end, despite all my mostly covert and manipulative resistances, we did sell up and move to Gloucester. My parents were not pleased but bowed to the inevitable as, indeed, did I.

A new chapter in my life had begun, a chapter that, on the surface, was completely new except that I had taken myself, that is, my Mask, to my new life.

13

I start again

This is how my life looked: new home, new neighbours, no friends and no job.

Turning to Jim for support he told me bluntly "I've got enough on my plate". So, yet again, I was left to sort out my life alone.

There weren't many secretarial jobs available. Then, one day, a leaflet came through the letterbox about a Government re-training scheme to improve job prospects. I decided to apply.

Little did I realise just what I was letting myself in for. It seemed just a question of filling in forms and checking which courses sounded interesting. I chose the postgraduate Diploma in Personnel Administration with no inkling about what such a programme entailed. I also knew nothing about Personnel Management. In fact, I only chose it because it had nothing to do with either computers or secretarial work, the other two options.

The implications of such a commitment only gradually dawned on me and I was overcome with anxiety. Throughout most of our ten years' marriage we had been a dual-income couple, so returning to full-time education meant that I'd need Jim's full support which, in fairness, he did give me. It would only be for a limited period of time but, initially, there was an intense guilt because my contribution made a significant difference to our lifestyle.

The thought of becoming a mature student was both incredibly daunting and immensely exciting. However, I didn't feel particularly confident about my academic potential. I kept remembering my London friends and how they found my comments amusing, even when I didn't mean them to be funny and this tended to confirm my self-perception of "charming but bubble-headed". All my life I had believed that, academically speaking, I didn't have what it takes, so I had to compensate by being particularly nice and fun to be with. And yet now, despite this self-perception, I still felt the unstoppable urge to go ahead with my application.

Once the grant was approved, I approached Bristol Polytechnic, the learning provider of the postgraduate course Diploma in Personnel Administration. This was 1976. Ron Webster, the programme organiser, interviewed me, spending an hour trying to assess the level of my education and compare it with equivalent British and French educational systems. He kindly pointed out the huge leap from where I was, academically speaking, and the programme I wanted to attend. He even asked me "How do you think you will manage to read academic books?" With pretend confidence I replied "I don't think that will be a problem at all!". I didn't tell him that, up until then, the extent of my reading had been women's magazines such as 'Woman', 'Woman's Own' and 'Woman's Weekly'.

He smiled, then thought for a while. Eventually he said, "Your best move would be to start with some 'O' and 'A' levels. Do 'O' level Maths, 'O' level Sociology and 'A' level Economics. If you pass the exams, come back and I will get you on the programme."

I went away absolutely elated.

The first thing I noticed on my first day at Gloucester College of Science and Technology was being surrounded by 16-17 year olds, who were absolutely fascinated by me. In turn, I was shocked at how conservative they were, particularly in terms of their expectations about how a married woman should be, think, act and look. I fitted none of their preconceived ideas. However, we all got along extremely well and I liked talking with them.

I gradually realised that my self-perception of "charming but bubble-headed" was false. As I attended classes and read academic books that I could actually follow, reflecting on what I was learning, I found out I actually had brains, an exhilarating discovery.

The whole experience had a deep impact, far beyond the subject being studied. It changed me and my self-perception, my curiosity was aroused and new feelings surfaced which I wanted to share with Jim.

Now his unresponsiveness began to matter even more, because I was bubbling over with excitement at learning and discovering so much, not only academically but also about myself.

Unfortunately, Jim seemed either unable to understand what was going on in my life or incapable of responding. Obviously, it was impossible for me to look inside him and really understand what he was feeling. All I knew was what he actually expressed aloud, which was very little. Deeply disappointed, I believed he just wouldn't make the effort; yet more evidence of how little he cared about me.

Being a full-time student was a revelation in more ways than one. I was not the only mature student in my Sociology class. Tony was about 5 years younger than me and we would spend our breaks together. For the first time ever I experienced somebody who was genuinely interested in what I had to say, my views and opinions. It was a heady time and perhaps not surprising that we became lovers. But it was more than sex. Not being listened to or feeling cared about had felt like an unsatisfied hunger for so long that, with his attention, I just blossomed.

My relationship with Tony soon ended and I focused back on Jim, still hoping he would some day show me the love I so craved.

Fortunately, my student life became increasingly thrilling and challenging. I discovered that the language of the various disciplines was distinctly British and male.

One example remains etched in my mind: studying for 'O' level Maths, the (male) teacher was using cricket terminology as the basis for mathematical calculations. I tried to explain to him that I had no idea what the terms meant but all he said was "that's your problem."

Not surprisingly, Maths, one of the subjects that Ron Webster had recommended, was giving me a lot of grief. It had also been my worst at school.

That's when Jim came into his own. I may not have been able to share my experiences with him emotionally but at a practical level he turned up trumps.

He spent hours patiently helping me with my homework and testing me afterwards, persisting despite my frequent displays of frustration at being slow to "get" it. I'm convinced that it's due to him that I achieved an A in 'O' level Maths, an absolutely amazing result. I also gained a B in 'A' level Economics, although I only just scraped through 'O' level Sociology.

These studies had taken nearly a year and I was now ready for the big time. I returned to Bristol Polytechnic triumphantly waving my exam results to show to Ron Webster and hold him to his promise of getting me onto the programme. To my dismay, he wasn't there, having taken a year's sabbatical. I had to compete just like everybody else and there were 200 applications for just 20 places.

It was a nail-biting time. I had never intended the 'O' and 'A' levels to be an end in themselves, rather, a stepping stone towards this particular programme.

Again, my parents, particularly Papi, tried to save me from myself but my Mask was so firmly fixed, I never explained to them truthfully how and why I felt as I did. Instead, I perversely kept them informed of progress towards my ultimate ambition. I was fuelling their anger and anxiety on the one hand and my own stress, guilt and resentment on the other.

Two weeks after the Polytechnic interviews, the big day finally arrived. I remember this one particular moment so well. The postman brought two letters – one from my parents, the other from the Polytechnic, which I opened first. I had been accepted. I practically whooped the house down with excitement. Then I opened my parents' letter. Papi had written, "by now you will have received a letter from the Polytechnic announcing that, regretfully, they are unable to offer you a place on the course. You have done all you could and it's time to get yourself a real job".

I regarded the fact that both letters arrived at the same time a breathtaking coincidence – one, opening up new horizons, and the other trying to close them down. In his effort to protect me, Papi was also trying to keep me small. That, I want to believe, was never his intention. The real reason Papi fought so hard against my desire for a career change was that I was challenging his judgement about what was right for me and the best way, in his view, of how I should live my life. He wanted me to look up to him the way Mami did and found it hard to accept my bid for independence, individuality and freedom.

In what they claimed were my 'best interests', they fought fiercely for the status-quo even going as far as writing directly to Jim, appealing to him to put a stop to "all that nonsense." They carried on their campaign even after I was accepted.

Papi, in particular, began to pile on the pressure. I had always given in to his logical arguments, unable to articulate my feelings. That had always been so, ever since I was a child.

Papi maintained that wanting something just because it really mattered to me was meaningless unless I could also explain why. But when this deep desire for something more stimulating than my secretarial work began to stir in me I knew that I simply had to follow my heart wherever it took me. Unfortunately, while I couldn't find the right words to convey my dream, Papi had always been able to explain very clearly why I should remain a secretary.

This time it was different. The greater the pressure Papi put on me, the more entrenched and determined I became, the complete opposite from my usual compliant self. Appealing directly to Jim for 'common sense' made me deeply resentful but never once did I let Papi know how I felt. All this so-called communication was by correspondence, taking 7-10 days each way. It also put Jim in an intolerable position and I deeply appreciated the fact that he gave me the time and space to do what I needed to do, never attempting to influence me one way or the other.

I had told my parents what my ultimate objective was, one to which Papi was fiercely opposed, arguing that, as a secretary, I already had significant experience but that, if I were to change careers, I would be a beginner at the ripe old age of probably 35 years or so by the time I started looking for a job again. I'd had my "little fling", as they called it, and it was now time to start "real life" again. Letters started "getting lost" once more. Another round of conflict began, even more bitter than the previous one.

This was something my parents, especially Papi, never understood. To them, the idea of abandoning security and job experience in favour of some dream was the utmost folly.

The next two years were such an eye-opener. I loved every minute of the programme. I used to spend a lot of time in the library and enjoyed the learning process so much that I actually dreaded the thought that it would soon end and I'd have to go back into the "real" world and find a job.

However, on the social side, I never stayed behind after class. The other students had formed themselves into groups but I just wanted to get back home. The remnants of my school days when I felt ill at ease in company were still with me.

The programme was assessed in part through written examinations and in part a project on the subject of our choice. I decided to examine the relationship between a secretary and her manager and found a placement at the Gloucester County Council where they gave me full access to their secretaries all delighted to be at the centre of some serious research.

The whole process of establishing the study parameters, doing research, designing a questionnaire, learning to carry out interviews, analysing the data and learning to write in an academic style was a steep learning curve. I put everything I had into it, working throughout the long summer months, and was absolutely thrilled to bits when I was one of only two to be rewarded with a 'Distinction'.

It was now 1978 and I was 33 years old. A whole new chapter of my life was about to begin.

That chapter wasn't quite as I had imagined. It was very hard to find a position in my chosen profession and after all the hurdles and hard work it looked as if my dream would be shattered.

Having come this far I wasn't giving up so easily, however, and I needed to find out what stood in my way.

Two factors were working against me: having no previous experience and not being professionally qualified as a Member of the Institute of Personnel Management which would mean another course of studies and more exams.

A new strategy was required. It was essential to find work as our finances had been pushed to stretching point. I found a secretarial position in Gloucester and, at the same time, enrolled on a distance learning programme to prepare for the Institute exams.

It was a good thing I didn't know in advance how challenging the road ahead was going to be.

14

My parents come to England

My parents wrote of the deteriorating political situation in Argentina. In those days there was always some crisis or other, but this time the Government had decided to buy off the Opposition by freeing the rents, previously frozen at artificially low levels under the Peronist regime. By freeing them in one fell swoop thousands of people would become homeless and my parents, now in their seventies, would also be affected.

Without a second thought we immediately brought forward a plan we had been toying with for many years, namely that Jim and I would bring my parents over to England to live near us. We would grow old together, as a family, and this crisis brought our plans well within our radar practically overnight.

I went home-hunting on their behalf, made enquiries with the Home Office and approached our mortgage lender for an increase in our mortgage. In short, I took over the whole project virtually single-handedly.

I found a flat that looked promising and negotiated a good price but, even so, it was a stretch. Still, at least we would be together again.

The day finally arrived: 2 September 1979. Together at last.

The sudden change in circumstances and subsequent frantic activity to beat my parent's eviction deadline meant I set aside some deep anxieties about having my parents that close again. Especially Papi who, although I loved him dearly, had always tried to impose his way of doing things.

The first thing I noticed was that, in Papi's presence, I reverted to my Buenos Aires days, inarticulate, unable to explain what I wanted or needed and what mattered to me.

My parents, for which read Papi, decided Saturdays were to be "Family Day". We would all have lunch and spend the afternoon together and that usually meant they would come to us. Initially, these family get-togethers were wonderful, there was so much catching-up to do but soon the novelty began to wear off.

It was during one of their visits when it happened, just two months after their arrival. Standing at the door saying our farewells, Jim commented on a lump he'd noticed at the side of Papi's neck. Papi replied that it had been there a while and didn't bother him at all. Jim said that had God meant him to have a lump there he would have been born with it – one of the least Jim-like comments I have ever heard come out of his mouth. I was amazed. Not only had he noticed the lump, which I hadn't, but he also expressed his concern in a firm yet sensitive way. I just didn't recognize this Jim.

Since Jim was so insistent, Papi humoured him and went to the doctor. All of us, including Jim, trooped into the doctor's office to hear the test results. I was glad Jim had taken the time off. The diagnosis was our worst nightmare: cancer, specifically a lymphoma. We just stood there, stunned. The doctor, seeing our state of shock spoke very gently, explaining that this type of cancer tends to happen in the elderly. Papi was 71. The treatment he proposed was a combination of radiation therapy and pills, i.e. chemotherapy.

It was hard on him but he followed it meticulously. Often he and I went to the hospital together and we had a great time, talking, making jokes, laughing while the other people in the waiting room glanced at us disapprovingly. Mami refused to believe we actually had a good laugh together. She imagined we would sit there overcome with doom and gloom. Instead, Papi was in good spirits except when he was in pain. Then he became angry and irritable lashing out at whoever was anywhere near him – usually Mami.

Things on the Plumtree front changed yet again in early 1980. Jim's job, which had brought us to Gloucester in the first place, was transferred back to Welwyn Garden City. Since I was doing distance learning at the time there was, technically speaking, nothing to stop me going back with him, nothing, that is, except one thing – intense guilt. We talked about me going with him but we knew it wasn't going to happen.

Jim commuted between Gloucester and Welwyn Garden City, getting back home on Friday evenings and returning on Monday mornings.

However, the fact that Jim and I were no longer together during the week did not deter Papi from seeking to preserve the "sanctity" of Family Day, limiting what little time Jim and I had together and causing both friction and a greater separateness between us.

During the week, this lifestyle worked well for me. I carried on with my secretarial work and then I'd go to my parents' flat where Mami cooked dinner for us. Afterwards, I studied.

However, it wasn't much of a life for either Jim or me and by early 1981 we were considering moving back together to Welwyn Garden City.

I had also been thinking about trying for a position on the lower rungs in Personnel Management. I struggled between my desire to be with Jim and staying near Papi. Jim, who had come to really care about my parents, also felt guilty about even thinking of my leaving them, especially now when Papi was so ill.

But, as time went on I was convinced that my place was with Jim. Then, to my surprise, he agreed. We just knew we couldn't carry on like that and decided to talk to my parents.

Papi was most upset. I was the apple of his eye and having me near meant everything to him but he had to recognise that husband and wife really should be together and agreed to let me go – on condition that I call them every single day.

Having come this far I would have agreed to anything so I gave my word, a promise I kept for many years.

15

Life takes on
a new turn

Jim and I entered a new phase in our marriage. We now had a common purpose to set up home together again and started house-hunting. Jim would select several houses for us to view and I'd travel down to London for the weekend. We always had a good time, going out for a film and a meal afterwards. We had lots to talk about and I felt closer to him than I had for years. I was really happy.

Eventually we found our dream home in Welwyn Garden City itself, located in a beautiful cul-de-sac called The Pastures, a conservation area. The price reflected the location, just above our budget but, as usual, once I'd set my heart on it, it was only a matter of time – and pressure – before Jim would be ready to give in. Moving-in day was 21 November 1981.

My next step was to find a job but, with my Personnel Management exams looming in June 1982 I decided to go for temping jobs, which paid very well. The Managing Director of one client was particularly taken with my language skills and offered me a permanent position at a top salary.

Again, my parents put me under intense pressure to forget my dream and accept that job. They appealed to Jim who, to his credit, refused to take sides or put me under pressure.

I bought myself time by assuring them that if I hadn't found a job in my field by a certain time, I would go back to secretarial work – a promise I had no intention of keeping.

By then I was very stretched, temping full time, studying for my exams and looking for jobs in Personnel Management.

Finally, after all those years, my hard work, persistence and determination were rewarded. I was offered a job as a Personnel Administration Manager with the charity Help the Aged – long before I reached that artificial "deadline".

The job paid a much lower salary than as PA to the Managing Director but the money meant nothing to me. All I knew was that I was about to step on the first rung of the ladder of my new profession.

Papi thought I was mad but, since he saw there was nothing that would make me change my mind he grudgingly gave in and actually wished me well.

In June 1982 I passed the exam, earning the right to use the letters MIPM after my name.

From then on my relationship with my parents actually improved and our bond became stronger. We tended to visit my parents every few months or so and during one of our visits Papi felt the need to talk about dying. It was constantly on his mind, he told us, but Mami refused to discuss it and would walk out of the room whenever he tried.

He then turned to us but Jim, unable to deal with it either, mumbled something along the lines of "don't be silly" and he, too, walked out of the room. That left me. I had always thought of myself as being at ease with the idea of death but, as I now discovered, only in the abstract; not when it touched me directly.

I did listen to him and I could see that being able to share his thoughts with me eased his burden, but it was transferred to me and I had no-one to share it with.

I felt overwhelmed, intensely sad and alone. I walked to Gloucester Cathedral and sat there for some time and that did help. Meanwhile, life awaited me in the shape of my dream job.

16

My new job

My job as Personnel Administration Manager was everything I had imagined it would be. I had the opportunity to put forward a series of ideas which were actually implemented. This required a lot of determination because the Personnel Manager, who had actually recruited me, hadn't expected me to take my job that seriously. His ethics and values, not to mention his integrity, were severely lacking and it was only with the support of my colleague Colin, the Recruitment Manager, that I managed to get my ideas across. Colin had the credibility I lacked as a woman.

My battle was to get my ideas implemented rather than to fight sexism and it was a strategy that paid off. When the Personnel Manager retired Colin was promoted to the role of Personnel Manager at Help the Aged and I was promoted to Personnel Manager of the sister charity, ActionAid, an international development agency.

Just when things were looking up for us financially, Jim was made redundant from Rank Xerox. This was 1984 and he was now 49 years old.

Redundancy completely demoralised him and the relentless rejections sapped his self-confidence. He put job searching on the back burner and declared that his chances would improve if he got a qualification in computer programming. Jim had supported me when I was studying for my own professional qualification and it was now my turn to support him.

Eighteen months later, having achieved his objective, he was back on the job market. Finding a job proved just as elusive as before, however, despite his qualification. Now 51, he became increasingly despondent and, eventually, gave up altogether.

This was very hard to deal with. He had been offered the services of a redundancy counsellor. She would give him tasks to do which he didn't carry out and, eventually, he stopped going.

I tried to be cheerful and upbeat but gradually I became impatient and resentful. I had supported us financially for nearly two years and still there was no indication that he wanted to change this arrangement. Meanwhile, I was settling into my new job. ActionAid had never had their very own Personnel Manager before and I was given carte blanche to recommend good practice to the Board. I had never felt so fulfilled, having found my niche.

In 1985 the Trustees decided to bring in a new Chairman – a bully who caused the biggest bloodshed in the history of the charity. He removed the Managing Director, demoted the Company Secretary who had been my immediate report and systematically went about destroying the confidence and morale of every single member of the Board and senior management team. Some came into my office after such sessions, shaking and white as a sheet.

My job changed beyond recognition and so did I. I became a nervous wreck, walking on eggshells. Jim was still unemployed so I tried to hang on. But it was not to be.

Giving me the sack was not an option because it would have constituted unfair dismissal. Instead, the Chairman offered me a payoff of six months salary to persuade me to resign. By then, my resistance had been well and truly sapped. For weeks I had been waking up in the mornings in tears, dreading going to work. I clung on because, I told myself, it fell on me to keep us going. I was terrified that if I allowed myself to be driven out of my job, we'd lose our home. The final battle lasted a few months, until March 1986 when all struggle and resistance had finally been eaten away.

Once it was all over I felt crushed and worn out. I sat around the house without any sense of identity and purpose, totally paralysed and unable to take any action and genuinely fearing no-one would ever employ me again.

Whilst in this vacuum all I could think of was how unfair the whole situation was, how I had not deserved what had happened to me. I kept turning things over and over again in my mind, wondering how I could have handled things differently and achieved a better outcome – no new director, no change, no loss of job, everything the way it was when life was beautiful, the birds sang, the sun shone and all was well with the world.

I soon rallied and realised that I really had to get a new job – and fast. I had been offered redundancy counselling, but couldn't accept the counsellor's suggestion to re-evaluate my talents, skills and genuine inclinations. The whole idea was a self-indulgent waste of time. I also knew exactly what my genuine inclinations were.

"All I need is your help to find another job; that's all I want", I insisted. Just one of my poorer choices.

I really tried to make job-searching a full-time "job" as my counsellor urged me to do, but by noon each day I had been to my local library, read all the newspaper ads, phoned for application forms, written application letters and had umpteen cups of coffee. Then the rest of the day stretched out interminably before me – with lots of time to worry about what the future would bring.

Jim, himself unemployed, was no help. I accused him of just sitting around, doing nothing. I'd shout at him to pull his finger out and try to find work but, at 51, he said he was too old for the market. As I continued to shout at him and cry helplessly, sobbing how scared I was, he would take me in his arms and try to reassure me. Something would turn up. His words sounded empty and meaningless.

We had no money coming in except for our unemployment benefit. I spent sleepless nights scared we might lose our home, but Jim didn't even try to help. His excuse about being too old didn't ring true. I knew there were companies who prided themselves that they hired people aged over fifty, although admittedly for low level work.

My resentment stemmed from when I had to postpone my dream of entering the personnel management profession and return to secretarial work because we needed the money so why couldn't Jim put himself out and help? It was a resentment that ate away at me for many years because he never worked again. His unemployment benefits stopped and only when he reached the age of 65 and received his pension did the financial pressure ease.

As the days passed and I had little to show for my efforts, I became less discriminating. I applied for any job that came up, however unsuitable. I would try to tease meaning out of the key words in the adverts to make them fit into my own experience and I had a few job interviews. As the outplacement programme included interviewing practice I fell back into my habit of "being all things to all people". The interviewers, particularly in smaller companies, were fairly inexperienced and under pressure to fill vacancies.

Eventually I did get a job offer which I promptly accepted. I was not about to change my tendency to stick my head in the sand, though, avoiding researching the job in case even I couldn't avoid recognising how unsuitable it was.

Only when it was too late did I realise the mistake I'd made. I was expected to deliver in an area for which I was totally ill-equipped in terms of skills, knowledge and experience.

I worked in the Personnel Department and one of the requirements was 'good communication skills'. Whilst I interpreted this as meaning 'interpersonal communications', they meant 'computer-literate'. This wasn't made clear at the interview. Internal politics also played a part. Eventually I got the sack.

Back where I started – unemployed and job-hunting – except that it wasn't quite where I started: I had changed.

I was talking with people, seeking advice, sharing experiences without pretending that I had it all under control and I stayed engaged with the outside world. I had greater confidence in the knowledge, skills and experience I had developed as Personnel Manager. I considered options that, only a few months earlier, I would have rejected out of hand. In between my job searching activities I took on some personnel and training projects on a freelance basis, which not only produced an income, albeit a small one, but also enabled me to come off State benefits – a huge morale boost.

I was invited to an interview for what seemed a very good position – around the same time I was also offered an interesting six month freelance project. I decided to check out both of them.

The job was less interesting than I had originally thought but it offered the security of (so-called) permanent employment. The project, on the other hand, although temporary, would enable me to use my skills and knowledge.

In the end I chose the route that was most unlike me – at least the 'me' I had believed myself to be, who played safe and stuck with the familiar, well within my comfort zone. I decided to go the freelance route – a way of life I kept up for the next 13 rollercoaster years.

17

Papi dies

In October 1988 my parents were approaching their big anniversary – 50 years of marriage. Jim and I travelled to Gloucester and we spent the day together. I asked them to sit together for a photograph. They were always uncomfortable being photographed but I'd insisted as it was such a special occasion.

As they sat there, rather stiff but holding hands, I called for a brief pause. They relaxed. Mami put her head on Papi's shoulder and he looked down at her with heart-stopping tenderness. I took the photograph – an indescribably loving moment captured on film.

Only two weeks later – Friday, 11 November 1988 – my Mum called. Papi had taken a turn for the worse and was in hospital. Without a second's hesitation I took the next train to Gloucester. It was a Friday evening. Mami had been with him since he was taken to hospital a few days back, only going home to feed the canaries and settle them for the night. Now we were able to take turns in staying with Papi and share some of the essential chores.

When he awoke Papi was delighted to see me. I kept him amused with stories about my job and colleagues which he enjoyed. But he was too tired to ask lots of questions. We encouraged him to rest and sat quietly with him.

On Saturday evening he was particularly bright but, instead of feeling encouraged I was anxious. That evening I phoned Jim and reported on Papi's state of mind. Then I said, "I don't know, I remember reading somewhere that people become fully alert just before they die". Jim replied, "Don't be silly" so I left it.

Mami and I spent Sunday at the hospital. Papi was sleeping and I was reading the papers all the while holding his hand. By 5:00 Mami said she would just pop back to the flat to see to the canaries, returning straight after. I nodded. Ten minutes went by.

I was still reading the papers when Papi's breathing changed, becoming increasingly laborious. I panicked and ran out of the ward shouting "help! help!", but there was no-one around. I then remembered what he'd recently told me, namely that he was ready to go. So I ran back and held him in my arms, loudly telling him (he had become hard of hearing) how much I loved him and that I would always look after

Mami. He shouldn't worry about her well-being. I kept repeating this until he stopped breathing altogether. I sat there for a few moments before I remembered that Mami was due back any minute now. He had actually died in the only fifteen minutes she had not been with him and I was glad it had worked out like that. I was relieved she didn't actually see him die.

I walked out of the ward and saw her coming along the corridor. We walked towards each other. She took one look at me and knew straight away, her face set like a mask. She didn't cry. It was Sunday, 13 November 1988.

In the weeks that followed I didn't really grieve much except every once in a while I would unexpectedly burst into tears. My main feeling, apart from loss, was one of tenderness, of completion as well as deep sadness. I had held him in my arms and told him how much I loved him. I felt at peace.

18

'Entre Nous' is born

One day in 1991, quite by chance, I bumped into Simone, a friend from earlier days. She specialised in PR and was looking for a different angle for her business. We went for a coffee to catch up with each other. I told her about my work as a trainer in business communication skills. She had recently established a dating agency. Together we came up with the idea of developing a workshop for single people, *'What to do when someone takes your fancy'*.

It was a snappy title that caught the media's attention and, with Simone's contacts, I was interviewed on television, radio and various magazines and newspapers. The hook was my being labelled as the 'flirting expert' and, although to me this was stretching it a bit, it was all just a bit of fun and I had a great time.

It was Simone who suggested that I write a book based on our workshop and eventually I produced *'Across A Crowded Room: How To Find And Keep The Love Of Your Life'*. Again, Simone's contacts enabled her to find a literary agent who organised a publisher. In July 1994, I signed a contract with Hodder Headline and received a substantial advance which Simone and I shared.

Having a book published and being in the public eye was absolutely thrilling and we had the time of our life.

Meanwhile, the label the media had stuck on me as the 'flirting expert' rang hollow at home. Jim and I remained generally out of synch when it came to sex and, over the years, he became less and less interested. I still cared for the closeness so, as before, I was always the one who took the initiative but it was lukewarm at best.

I kept persisting because I had created this fantasy that Jim really loved me but I felt rejected by his lack of interest. Over the years it eroded my self-perception as an attractive woman.

19

My mask stops
working

Despite the positive changes I had made to my life through my own efforts there was still space for long-forgotten feelings to come to the surface.

The excitement of my new book, of being on radio and television, highlighted just how empty and one-sided my relationships felt. And yet I knew no other way of making them more fulfilling other than try even harder to be "nice", "charming" and "fun to be with". I thought my new-found celebrity status would change the way I felt about myself, but it made no difference. I blindly continued to behave the same way as before.

I continued to believe that the Mask I presented to the outside world worked reasonably well: I tended to be popular because I was easy-going and never critical – except with Jim. I never, ever, made a stand. Not even when I didn't like what was going on or what was said, however sexist, racist or bigoted, deliberately offensive or hurtful or even merely thoughtless. I simply had no boundaries.

There would have been plenty of opportunities to make a stand whilst rubbing shoulders with the media, but I avoided any conflict, fearing interview invitations would cease.

However, slowly – very slowly indeed – something began to shift.

I noticed a sense of discomfort in certain situations and around certain people, a discomfort I couldn't pin down. I disliked being described as a nice person – something I used to regard as a compliment. I knew in my heart that my niceness was not genuine. Often I was pretending to be pleasant and agreeable when inside I felt quite different. Much of my behaviour was driven by fear of loss or purely a means to win a project.

I actually began to "hear" it when someone exclaimed in exasperation: "why can't you just be yourself!" or say, dismissively, "you're too good to be true". Such comments always left me feeling helpless and frustrated, not comprehending what was wanted of me. Had I known, I would instantly have given it.

I dimly saw that all my contortions, intended to avoid or minimize risk of rejection, created exactly the opposite effect.

The rejections weren't always spelt out, but couched in frequent excuses, such as

"I'm very busy right now" for weeks on end, or "my life has totally changed and I'm moving to a different part of the country."

Over the years, some "friends" stopped returning my calls. Feeble excuses did nothing to reassure my fragile sense of belonging and I learned nothing that would have helped me understand.

I used to complain that people didn't take me seriously, I was taken for granted, not listened to, my needs ignored and so on. After so many years of projecting my image as charming, agreeable, a good sport, unconditionally supportive, always cheerful – most definitely always cheerful – I literally lost touch with my Real Self. The Mask I wore, my survival mode, my False Self, was who I had become.

Yet despite all these new insights I still didn't know how to produce another outcome.

20

It is crunch time

It was now 1992. My loneliness drove me into the arms of Roger. I found it nothing short of amazing to again meet a man who really listened to me, liked me. Not only that, who also fancied the hell out of me – and me of him. All my deepest needs were being met. It was enough to make me forget my previous struggles and insights.

Roger had recently separated from his wife but missed his young son. The separation was to be temporary and I decided to be there for him while he sorted things out. I had no intention of leaving Jim, so the arrangement suited both of us.

The early stage of our relationship was wonderful. I could share my innermost feelings, hopes and dreams with him and he would share his. He had a business idea but had trouble putting it across to potential clients. I would listen to his pitch and then we would work together to hone his message. An important need of mine was being met – to be there for another person, be able to make a difference and to have that same person actively share in the things that mattered to me.

Over time, however, our relationship gradually became less intense until it just chugged along sporadically for a couple of years with me, as usual, being the one to engineer our meetings and he just going along with it. Roger was struggling both with his business and trying to find a way back to his family, but it wasn't working out. I turned a blind eye to the change in our relationship because I believed us to be friends, but he became less communicative and finally I saw his feelings had simply fizzled out and I hadn't wanted to notice.

Eventually, he took the initiative. "It's me, not you", he said lamely and extended a lifeline "but we can stay friends".

I suspected there were things he wasn't telling me and took it very personally. I'd done everything I could to make it work – given as much of myself as I knew how, not been (too) demanding, and always supportive and loving. Desperate to keep the relationship going I carried on being cheerful, undemanding, supportive and agreeable and he passively went along. The affair limped on a few weeks longer.

Then I picked up a marketing blurb for a workshop called "Communicating with

Emotional Integrity".

This was July 1994, 2 year after I met Roger and, although I didn't know it, my life was about to change.

21

I meet Alan,
my life coach

My affair was on its last legs yet I was still hanging on. When I read the description of this workshop it touched something in me.

I immediately booked a place. I just knew this was what I had been looking for. A saying kept going round and round in my head: 'When the student is ready, the teacher appears'.

I was certainly ready and couldn't wait to get started but my cheque was returned because the workshop was cancelled due to lack of interest.

I couldn't believe it. I was devastated: So sure my life was about to change and then the door slams in my face. I admit it: I am a drama queen (I was going to say 'a bit of a drama queen' but that wouldn't begin to do it justice.)

I couldn't let it rest. I called the organisers to find out who the tutor on that course was – I wanted his name, his address, his phone number – anything that would enable me to track him down.

And eventually I did. He was Alan Bec and lived in Nottingham. That made me pause. I lived in Welwyn Garden City; he, in Nottingham. That wasn't much use to me.

I left it – but "it" wouldn't leave me. In the end I gave in; it was as if something was driving me to get in touch with him. Nothing like that had ever happened to me before. Trying to make sense of it all I reasoned that, since we were both trainers, perhaps we could work together in some way. Again, in what way I didn't know. In the end I couldn't put it off any longer and called him.

To put this into context, it's worth mentioning the kind of person I was. My belief was that, if I couldn't see it, touch it, taste it, hear it or feel it with my physical body – it didn't exist. I knew nothing of, and had certainly not given any thought to, the unseen world, never reflected on such things as drives, energy, atmosphere, the power of truth, how attitudes, values and beliefs create our reality, issues around perception and interpretation, and much more besides. Goals and checklists were the things I understood and used to make my plans move forward – except when they didn't. Only thought and reason made any sense to me because they were things I understood and, therefore, made me feel in control.

Now fast forward to this moment when I finally knew I simply had to call this man.

We talked. I asked when he planned to come to London next. He had no such plans. I pushed. He was unmoved. We talked some more. We left it that I would call again in a few weeks to see if his plans had changed.

Eventually, after several phone calls, he told me he was coming to London on business and we arranged to meet. A few days beforehand I called him to confirm we were still on track. He asked "Is there something you would like me to bring?"

"Nothing", I replied, "just bring yourself – I only know that I simply have to talk with you and I have no idea why. Isn't that weird?"

"It isn't weird at all", Alan said, "it happens to me all the time."

"But it doesn't happen to me!" I exclaimed.

"Well", he observed, "it just did, didn't it?"

That stopped me in my tracks. It was true – it never did, and now it had.

We met. He talked about "energy", "atmosphere and presence", "the power of the unseen" and something about the process of change. It was all gobbledygook to me. Yet for some reason I thought: "I want this" even though I had no idea what exactly "this" actually was; I just knew it was important.

At that time, my main concern was that I had very few clients and attracting new ones was proving very difficult. This was causing me endless sleepless nights worrying about financial survival or, to put it more accurately, destitution.

"What I need", I explained, "is your help in finding more clients."

He then dangled a tantalising carrot in front of me. "When you change", he said, "your whole life will change."

I told him of the affair, more in the spirit of "see how resourceful I am when it comes to meeting my needs? And, anyway, I'm not taking anything away from Jim".

Alan was not impressed. He pointed out that our work together was to be a journey towards truth, integrity and authenticity, and that having an affair was the exact opposite. He made it clear that, if I didn't end the affair he would not be prepared to work with me. I ended the affair. This was hard for me. I knew my relationship with Roger was not love, but it was all I had.

During one of our early meetings Alan asked me a question.

"What are you feeling right now?"

I looked at him blankly.

"Feeling?" I repeated puzzled.

"Yes", Alan said, "What are you feeling? For example, are you feeling hot or cold or what?"

Still not understanding I shrugged.

"I feel fine", I replied, not sure where he was going. He didn't say anything further and we dropped it.

With my clients' agreement Alan started by shadowing me in my business meetings and accompanied me to television studios where I was being interviewed about my so-called expertise in flirting.

I loved the glamour of being in the media. Imagine, me on the telly! I was sure Alan would be deeply impressed. He wasn't dealing with just anybody! No, sir!

Alan was indeed impressed – just not in the way I hoped.

It didn't take long for me to recognise how deeply important my work with Alan was and, despite my financial struggles I knew only this: I would beg, steal or borrow but nothing would make me stop my work with him, slow and demanding as it was. I felt my life was at stake and, even if it does sound dramatic, it was. My work with him was offering a life that was meaningful and fulfilled rather than merely existing as I had done so far. My meetings with him always ended with my experiencing a mixture of inner turbulence and hope.

I began to learn about my self-image and how it influenced the way I saw myself. I liked to think I was a sanitised version of my True Self and it was this sanitised version that I presented to the world.

As Alan started holding up the mirror, showing me who I really was – as opposed to who I liked to believe I was – I took the first steps on a road littered with defensiveness, struggle and resistance. What I really wanted was for my life to change without the battle of having to change myself.

"You don't have to do anything", Alan told me, "All you need to do is observe". When I asked him what I was supposed to observe, he replied, "Everything!"

Being told that I didn't have to do anything to change made me feel really helpless; all I'd ever known was that, if I wanted to achieve a particular objective then I needed to do something in order to get there. And now, here he was, suggesting I didn't have to do anything at all. Scary. I felt helpless and out of control.

I brought a long agenda to our sessions, a list of things I wanted to talk about. But he kept encouraging me to forget agendas and talk about whatever mattered to me. I was really afraid that I would forget something important but Alan kept assuring me that nothing would ever get lost.

"Whatever bothered you a week or so ago when you prepared the list", he'd say, "will keep coming up until we deal with it."

Yet I kept hanging on to them because they made me feel in control and, therefore, safe. Alan wasn't in the business of making me feel safe. He eventually succeeded in weaning me off my agendas and I learnt to trust myself enough to know what mattered to me at the time we actually met. I finally understood that whatever was buried deep inside of me would come up again and again until we examined and dealt with it. As he'd rightly said, nothing would get lost.

One of my ongoing complaints was that people didn't take me seriously, they took me for granted, didn't listen to me and ignored my needs. As Alan continued to hold up the mirror, I could see that it was me who was taking myself for granted, who didn't take myself seriously or listen to myself, that I ignored my needs, sabotaged and betrayed myself.

As I gradually learned to observe 'everything' I also started to pay attention to my thoughts, my feelings, the things I said and did and how people reacted and responded. As I slowly became better at noticing, I also became aware of the clues to the state of my life through an unexpected ally: my body.

22

How my body proved
to be my ally

The exciting times around the publication of my book, the workshop and being in the eye of the media could not disguise the effects of the many upheavals and stresses I had experienced since arriving in England. The legacy of those years led to a range of episodes of poor health, none of which seemed related to each other.

I'd go to the doctor but my symptoms seemed disconnected. Over the years I experienced lower back pain, sharp pain in my wrists, itchy eyelid, the vision of my left eye trembled, I experienced intense pain in the region of my ovaries, disabling pain in the left knee, sharp stomach cramps and various other conditions.

The GPs I consulted over the years each dealt with the symptoms separately and, in most cases they prescribed painkillers. Some arranged a variety of tests and experimented with different medicines. Nothing worked and different symptoms kept emerging over the years. Finally, I gave up trying to find a connection and just dealt with whatever I was experiencing in the best possible way, trying both conventional and alternative approaches. Most the time the symptoms disappeared of their own accord.

I developed a profound belief in "mind over matter". I had always regarded it as a weakness to give in to my body and, therefore, I'd push myself almost beyond my own limits before I'd admit defeat and stay at home from work. This had partly to do with my upbringing, never being allowed to stay home from school, however much I complained about feeling unwell; only if the school sent me back home was I "allowed" to be ill.

But there was more, something quite insidious. There was a story Mami would tell me about Papi when I was a child, going back to the days when they were forced to live in the jungles of Bolivia.

Papi was working for the local council in one of the villages in the Yunga (a wild forest). They were improving the provision of electric lighting to a network of villages. Papi was the capataz in charge of the project. One morning on his way to work, he accidentally stepped on a rusty nail. As Mami tells it, he was not daunted and not only did he continue to walk to his place of work, he never even got a blood infection.

Mami always regarded Papi as a true hero and she loved him beyond measure.

This story highlighted the kind of man he was, deserving of huge admiration. As a child, the story imparted the subliminal message not to give in to my body – so I too became a "hero". I had to be a hair's breadth from keeling over before I was prepared to take time out.

The other clue my body gave me over many years were prolonged periods of uncontrollable crying. I used to wonder that my body actually held so much water. Individual episodes would last as long as several weeks.

At first the severest bout of crying happened around February, providing me with the excuse that it had something to do with winter, a time when most people experience sadness or depression.

Gradually it happened more often, putting paid to that little theory. However, I genuinely believed that I had no idea what the trigger or the reasons were.

Alan persevered in helping me see the real cause of my sadness, which I continued to deny.

For a long time, whenever I was due to meet Alan, I would feel the strongest urge to cry. I would hold on until we were together as only then did I feel safe enough to let go.

Alan kept bringing up the state of my marriage, yet I persistently refused to even discuss it, despite the fact that my body continued to offer me clues with copious tears and episodes of the deepest sadness.

I remember one particular session that highlights the strength of my resistance. On that day, my body felt as if it were going to explode under the strain of holding back my tears. Alan and I had arranged to meet at a coffee place. I arrived early and sat at one of the corner tables choosing a seat facing the wall with a pile of tissues at my elbow.

Soon after Alan arrived I started to sob and, as usual, declared that I had no idea why I felt so wretched.

Alan started to review choices I'd made in my life.

"Are you sad because you chose not to have children?"

"No", I replied.

"Do you feel lonely?",

"No", I said again.

"Are your friendships superficial and unfulfilling?"

"No", I repeated.

Finally he came to the state of my marriage and my relationship with Jim.

"Are you unhappy with Jim?", he asked.

"No".

He paused.

There was nothing more left to say.

One of Alan's statements that I did manage to hear was that "the only way to deal with sadness – or anything else for that matter – is by going through it, not around it as you've been trying to do all these years. If you try to avoid or go around it, it will come back again and again until you deal with it".

I was equally struck by Alan's questions about whether or not I had relationships in my life that caused me hurt and pain. A rather strong way of putting it, I thought. Reflecting, I concluded there wasn't anyone in my life that made me feel that I wasn't good enough. Even though I genuinely believed it to be true, I knew that Alan would disagree with this assessment.

It took me a long time to understand that by ignoring those messages I was creating distance not only between myself and others but also between my False Self and the real me. This made me feel empty and alone.

23

My relationship
with myself

While I was complaining about whatever was going wrong for me at the time, Alan commented, "People live the lives they love, irrespective of what they say."

I thought that was very unfair – more, it was a shocking thing to say – no, even more than that, it was outrageous. I was angry.

However, once I climbed down from my high horse I had to – grudgingly – admit the truth of it, certainly in the context of my own life.

I finally allowed myself to see that, unintentionally, I had sabotaged the things I said I wanted the most and the relationships I said I valued most highly. Being in control and being right were more important to me than being happy and at peace with myself. Although my body was telling me that being in control and being right gave me no sense of security or happiness I was too inexperienced to recognise these sensations for what they were: messages from my Real Self.

In the continuing pursuit of control I developed mechanisms that were really effective in keeping people at a distance, despite the fact that I wanted the exact opposite.

One way was being a people-pleaser and putting other people's needs ahead of my own. Although this seems to contradict my efforts to try and manipulate others not only into doing what I wanted them to do but also doing things my way, to me it actually made perfect sense.

The reason why these techniques seem to contradict themselves is because I had needs that were at odds with each other, such as the need to be liked which clashed with the need to be in control. Since I believed that to be liked required me to refrain from openly expressing my real needs the only way to meet them, I believed, was to resort to covert measures – hence manipulation and control.

However, none of my contortions produced the outcome I so deeply longed for – to be loved. Worse, by denying my needs, combined with attempts at manipulating to get them met, I actually contrived my own disempowerment.

Another approach was trying to change people who did not fit my expectations and fantasies, as I had been doing with Jim for all these years.

However, my repertoire of techniques for keeping myself isolated extended even further and was founded on a variety of beliefs such as 'they'd be bored with me if they knew how I really felt', 'they couldn't handle my real feelings', 'I don't want to worry them', 'I don't want to be a burden' and 'I can handle it'. Beneath each of these beliefs was a more fundamental one – that I was unworthy of love and support.

But there was more; I didn't want people to see that I felt vulnerable or that I was unsure of myself because I thought they needed to know I was strong – I was the one who needed people to believe I was strong which, as I mentioned before, meant being a "hero".

All that required me to stay away from friends when I was experiencing a rough ride and only talk about it afterwards, for example, over dinner and a glass of wine. Then it made an entertaining story.

When someone challenged me I would become defensive and go on the counter-attack to deflect the criticism and turn it on the other person. That was another useful strategy that enabled me to avoid looking at myself. I used to do this a lot with Jim, often saying to him accusingly, "On whose side are you anyway!"

Minimising something by joking about it was another handy mechanism and light-heartedness at all costs was my trademark. All these tactics were highly successful in helping me create a lonely and empty life. I knew I felt lonely; I just didn't realise I was the one creating the emptiness I was complaining about.

I suppose Alan was right: people do create the life they love whatever they may say or, to put it more accurately, whatever I might say.

When I first started working with Alan, more often than not I was afraid of letting go of my old values and beliefs because to do so would be to admit that I'd got it wrong – even if, as it was becoming increasingly clear, those values and beliefs no longer served me.

As I continued to struggle and resist, Alan gave me a book to read called "The Teachings of Don Juan" by Carlos Castaneda, in which he describes his journey to becoming a Shaman. In it I found a section that crystallised for me what I was putting myself through.

Don Juan, a Yaqui Indian with supernatural powers, a sorcerer, who took on Carlos Castaneda as his disciple speaks to Carlos about his continual struggles and resistances, always trying to understand what cannot be understood. Carlos' fear was that, if he stopped struggling and resisting, it would mean surrender. This is what Don Juan said:

"You want to cling to your arguments despite the fact that they bring nothing to you; you want to remain the same even at the cost of your well-being."

That was exactly what I was putting myself through. I wanted my life to change without me having to change in the process. What I really wanted was for everybody else to change, not me, so I continued to blame others for the unsatisfactory state of my life and my relationships, and I continued to look outwards for happiness and security. In fact, I kept holding on for dear life to my False Self, that very False Self that was the source of the poverty of my life.

My greatest fear was that opening myself up to changing would require me to surrender control and, if there was one thing I believed was central to my survival it was to keep tight control over as many areas of myself and my life as I could.

Even the idea of letting go of that control terrified me – fear of the unknown, fear of the unforeseen, coming face-to-face with some unexpected or unimaginable consequences, fear of rejection, fear of looking foolish, fear of making myself vulnerable, fear of being helpless – fear, fear and more fear. I was afraid to open what I regarded as Pandora's Box because I didn't know what lurked within. This fear had always been true for me even when I refused to admit it to myself.

For many years before I met Alan and for many years after I was constantly afraid, particularly of destitution and of losing my home. Most of the time I felt as if I were living at the edge of a precipice. Nights were the worst. I'd wake up at two or three in the morning overcome with terror. I had this little phrase that neatly summed up this terror: "next stage is cardboard city" where the down-and-outs and the homeless live using cardboard boxes to keep themselves warm. There was nothing in between for me.

I never, ever considered that the outcome might not be this dark, threatening cloud that could, in the blink of an eye, turn into devastating reality. The fear of destitution was the sword of Damocles hanging over my head.

Furthermore, every fear had a 'because' attached to it which gave it life by making it feel real and plausible. "I am afraid of (whatever) because of (this very good reason)", I would tell myself. Some of my friends actually accused me of "catastrophising" which I would strenuously deny because, I insisted, my fears were real.

Being in a constant state of fear had deep consequences, particularly in the way I communicated with myself and others although, at the time, I couldn't see the connection.

For example, fear led me to compromise myself by accepting work that wasn't in my best interests, from people I didn't trust and that caused me stress. As a self-employed person I never felt able to say 'no' to whatever work was offered, even when it was outside my area of competence.

Fear led me to tie myself into knots in order to please, be acceptable and be accepted. I ignored my own intuitions because of possible conflict with people I thought I needed and was afraid of living without.

Of course, when confronted with the way I lived my life, I denied it was fear. My denials didn't change the one unavoidable consequence: that I was sabotaging myself in all areas of my life – my finances, my relationships, the way I earned my living.

But my body knew because I was exhausted all the time: hiding from the truth and keeping up pretences is deeply exhausting.

24

I take my mask off
– a little at a time

There finally came the point when a part of me knew that I no longer wanted to live life this way. However, this wasn't a conscious decision and my resistance meant that not even Alan could help change my life all at once as, according to books I've read over the years, other people have done.

In my case, it was more a matter of taking my Mask off a little at a time. I would concentrate on one aspect of my life, experience significant learning and positive change, and then move on to another aspect as if it were completely new.

I had been self-employed for thirteen years, a period of considerable financial insecurity.

It was now 1998 and, luckily, I had managed to drop one of my particularly damaging habits, pretending I was doing well when I wasn't in order to protect my self-image. I told people what was really going on, not necessarily because I expected anything from them but more in the spirit of being open and truthful.

I told my friend Michael about my struggle to find new clients. He too experienced similar problems in his small debt-collection agency. We agreed to help one another. My job was to phone large consultancies and arrange meetings where Michael (and sometimes I) would make presentations. The aim was to get them to outsource their work to us. He was only able to pay me £30 per day and could afford three days a week, but it helped pay the mortgage.

I really enjoyed working with Michael, learning a new skill and feeling I was making a contribution.

25

I experience long
forgotten feelings

Then I experienced a breakthrough. I was reading a novel when, without warning, I burst into tears. Whilst sobbing my heart out, quite unexpectedly, memories of my childhood came flooding back. Things Papi used to say to tease me, causing me pain which I'd suppressed for all these years. I was now re-experiencing all the hurt and resentment. And it was as if the floodgates had opened and I was inundated by wave upon wave of pain. This lasted for weeks. I tried to tell Jim but he didn't know what to say, so I told Mami. That was not a good idea because she became very upset, insisting that I'd got it all wrong. I said she could not argue about my feelings and that her memories weren't mine. I knew she minded terribly because her memories of my childhood tend to be on the idealistic side, yet I couldn't stop talking about it.

Several months went by. I was in the middle of reading a novel when something triggered a sudden understanding of the forces that had shaped Papi – his childhood, his own parents' neglect and his isolation and loneliness. I felt overwhelmed with compassion for him. It was as if that feeling of compassion scoured me clean of all the pain and resentment that had burdened me for the past few months. I was healed. It took much longer for Mami to understand but, eventually, she did.

Alan acknowledged the progress I'd made and asked,

"And when was the last time you felt really angry?"

I laughed. I actually laughed. I really thought the idea that I might feel anger rather funny.

"I'm not angry", I exclaimed, "I'm never angry!"

The idea was preposterous. Alan let it go.

It was not long before I had the opportunity to test this assumption. The experience was so intense that it is indelibly etched on my mind.

Michael and I were on the train together on our way to meet a client. The day before I'd had an argument with him and was still feeling unsettled since, for me, the issue had not been resolved.

Gradually I became aware of a rage so intense that I had to acknowledge it had little to do with my argument with him, although I had no idea where it was coming from. I had never experienced such rage before and it became so strong that I felt my body would not be able to hold it. I could hardly breathe and I wanted to scream and sob and run away – none of which was possible since we were sitting on a train. Meanwhile, the energy swirling around inside of me made me feel as if I was going to explode any second.

The only thing I knew was that I needed to talk with Alan and I called him the minute we arrived at our destination. Fortunately, he was in and the minute he answered I started to sob into the phone, unable to speak. He waited for me to calm down.

"If you had to tell someone how you feel", he asked, "what would you say?"

And what came out of my mouth was:

"Stop hurting me!". I stopped, shocked. I had no idea who was hurting me.

It was only years later that I came to the conclusion it was Jim. Later still I finally arrived at the truth. It was me who had been hurting myself – by accepting the unacceptable, allowing outdated beliefs to drive my choices about how I should live my life – choices that caused deep damage, anger and resentment to the point of (suppressed) rage for many years.

Finally reaching the point of this realisation was a slow and convoluted process. Meanwhile, that day, I still had to find a safe way to defuse my rage and I finally resolved it by finding a park to run in until I was totally spent. Of course, that was only a temporary measure but a very useful one.

Then I started noticing various unkind behaviours from Jim. I had often experienced them over the years, but I persisted in reassuring myself that he was just distracted or forgetful. Here's an example: like everybody else, I have some preferences about how I like things to be. For instance, taking the bus home after shopping Jim, who would be carrying the shopping bag, put it on the floor. I always made it absolutely clear that the bag was not to be placed afterwards on the kitchen counter – it was unhygienic and I hated it. However, if I wasn't alert, that's exactly where it would go – even after years and years of me telling him repeatedly.

It took years before I realised that he was doing it deliberately and I confronted him.

Having spent most of my adult life pretending I never felt anger or rage, my work with Alan gradually began to bring these feelings to the surface, so I could find a safe way to express them however uncomfortable I might feel doing so.

Interacting with anonymous individuals in call centres can often trigger my anger. They are trained to respond to legitimate complaints from a script and do not deviate even if the earth were to crumble around them. Such experiences leave me screaming inside – and sometimes, I admit, at them – with frustration, impotence and rage, while they remain totally unmoved.

I remember one particular occasion. I had been carrying stress and anger for a few weeks until the rage finally erupted – I was at home on my own, having just finished yet another unproductive conversation. Again I called Alan. He explained that the reason for my physical distress was the adrenaline sloshing about in my body with nowhere to go. As an emergency measure he suggested that I shout at my plants.

"They'll wither away and die!", I wailed.

"On the contrary", Alan reassured me, "they love being shouted at".

Despite myself I had to laugh. They turned out to be very loving and patient listeners, hearing me out whilst I let off steam.

Alan also explained why I experienced such intense rage. Because I'd allowed my initial, fairly mild feelings of frustration to remain unexpressed, the longer the situation remained unresolved and unexpressed the greater my pent-up anger, until I believed I would really go wild.

The answer, he suggested, was to express my feelings – all of my feelings – when they actually come up rather than keeping them to myself. I found it really hard to follow this simple advice. Crying was the only acceptable way for me to express my deepest feelings of anger, helplessness and frustration.

26

I return to
corporate life

Money was the focus of my fears, being fundamental to our survival. Fear of 'not having' dominated my life.

Eventually the point came when, however much I enjoyed working with Michael, I needed to earn a decent salary.

Being truthful with people was what brought about the opportunity for a job in my current company.

My role was newly-created and an experiment. The work involved selling courses, programmes and professional qualifications to directors and senior executives. This new challenge gave me a real thrill.

Selling on the phone didn't fit in with my self-image though. I was really a Trainer (with a capital T) and not a saleswoman, despite the grand title of Client Development Executive.

Initially my status was self-employed consultant, though, which fitted in with my delusion that I was still a trainer with lots of training work to come. I never let reality get in the way of my fantasies.

A few months into the job my friend John, who had alerted me to this position originally, was promoted to Head of my department. I soon suggested that he employ me on a full-time basis.

"Are you sure this is what you really want?", he countered, "You've been telling me all these years that you never want to become employed again".

Eventually I convinced him and in September 1999 my position was formalised.

Still, I did miss my training work which I secretly regarded as a more worthy profession than selling courses on the phone and I said to Alan, "I can't imagine having been put on this Earth to make phone calls and sell!" my voice filled with disdain.

I was in a state of conflict because whilst I really enjoyed the work I also felt it wasn't really "good enough". I hadn't been able to earn an adequate living offering my training skills but was reluctant to face that reality.

Alan's response to my comment was: "It doesn't matter what you do; all that matters is how you do it."

Such a powerful statement! In an instant my pre-conceptions were turned upside down. At last I had grasped that when I genuinely care about my work and my colleagues I create a fulfilling work environment that spills over into my life as a whole.

I loved this job. I loved the fact that I was good at it and especially loved the fact that I had a regular income, paid holidays and sickness absence, medical insurance and a Pension! I especially appreciated being paid holiday and sick leave – something all employed people take for granted but the self-employed don't enjoy. I also loved the fact that I was surrounded by people instead of working mostly on my own at home. Until then, I hadn't really appreciated how isolated I'd been.

What had started as an experiment with me turning up a few times a month worked out so well that two more people were hired and John offered me the position of Team Leader.

I was thrilled. I remember thinking: "I want to prove to John that he's made the right decision." This apparently innocuous and outwardly positive thought was, in fact, a deeply destructive one. Like the millions of similar thoughts that preceded this one, it led me to do whatever I thought it took to please him and to prove to him that he was right to choose me for the job.

It didn't take long before things started to go wrong. The Team Leader's role was nothing like I imagined it. I had less time on the phone, which I really missed, and spent hours at management meetings.

One of my first tasks was to write a report about the sales team strategy for the coming year. I didn't know how to think or plan at a strategic level. In fact, I didn't really know what a strategy was. I was petrified at the prospect of being found out and getting more stressed by the minute.

One of my colleagues, Jon, saw me struggling. He came over and asked "Would you like me to help write the report?" It was help I would have loved to accept. Instead, I replied "No, thank you, Jon. I'm fine. I can handle it." I turned him down because I was afraid he was after my job. I couldn't admit to any uncertainty because that would have exposed my self-doubts. I even bought a book about business report writing which proved less than useless. Actually, it could have provided me with one or two helpful ideas but my anxiety was so overwhelming that I simply couldn't think straight. And so, I painted myself into a corner, pretending that I was in control and that all was well – even though it clearly wasn't. Everyone could see through me yet I still tried to keep up the pretence.

27

Pain and self-deception

As my episodes of severe lower back pain making my life anything from uncomfortable to miserable kept resurfacing the best advice my GP had to offer was that I would have to learn to live with it. I genuinely came to believe that there was nothing I could do to help myself. Because lower back pain is such a common condition, surrendering my personal power to a higher authority (my GP) fitted well with the aspect of my Mask called "being a hero".

I barely managed to commute to work, do my job and commute back home again. Painkillers only worked temporarily and there is, after all, a safety limit.

Talking to a friend about it, she made a suggestion that struck me as bizarre.

"Ask yourself", she suggested, "what the pain is trying to tell you. See if you can associate it with any particular emotion."

Over the next couple of days, as I was walking to the station, I reflected on this. Unexpectedly, a word sprang to mind: "Impotence". That was nonsense and didn't mean anything. I decided to try again. The word that came to me was "Hopelessness".

Since neither one of these two words made any sense to me I set the whole thing aside or, at least, I tried to. I was intrigued but had no idea what it all meant.

In the end, I asked Alan and his response really shocked me to the core.

"You have been in 'hopelessness' and 'impotence' ever since I met you", he pointed out, "When you are in "impotence" you believe that there is nothing you can do about whatever the situation happens to be at the time, and "hopelessness" is your belief that it will be like this forever."

The recognition was immediate and the clarity, blinding. It was true. This is what I have always believed in every single challenging situation, in every area of my life, not just health.

Once I recognised what I was doing to myself – playing the victim – I decided to take responsibility. I began by taking a good look at my routines.

I experimented to see what actions, activities, body postures and even emotional states made my back pain feel worse or better and then waited to see how my back responded to each of the changes.

Probably the most significant change I introduced into my routine was to stop getting in to work half an hour before I actually had to. As a sales person I didn't have a lot of work to do that early in the morning but it made me feel virtuous. Instead, I went to a Starbucks round the corner; I would sit there, sip a mocha, read or sometimes simply gaze into the middle distance and listen to the background music. It made an enormous difference to my readiness to start my working day. But the greatest success in dealing with my back pain came from going to a McTimoney chiropractor called Aarti Shah, a specialist to whom my doctor had referred me and who made a huge difference to both my pain levels and general well-being.

Poor health has proved to be a fertile learning ground, highlighting my negative and often self-destructive habits and beliefs. The belief, for example, that I must be unfailingly reliable and never, ever let other people down. I believed that being strong and a "hero" are the same thing and I now could see how I used this self-styled heroism as a mechanism to create distance between myself and other people (because "heroes" don't "whinge"). I created loneliness and emptiness because I didn't allow anyone to support me, either physically or emotionally. It was not that I didn't need it or want it but because I never asked for it. And I never asked for it because "heroes" can handle it!

I had come to interpret "surrender" as a dirty word. To me, "surrender" meant "giving up" or, worse, "giving in". If I'm not able to portray myself as "strong" then I will become a burden, people will be put off by me and my life will be lonely and empty. The fact that my life already felt lonely and empty didn't affect that belief one little bit.

I made another astonishing discovery whilst Alan and I were having one of our sessions. As Alan shone the metaphorical torch onto yet another one of my distorted beliefs, I was in a place of acceptance instead of my usual defensiveness and resistance. I acknowledged the point he made then stopped, struck by a flash of insight.

"Wait a minute", I said, "haven't you said this before?"

"Yes", Alan replied, "many times."

Up until that moment I would have sworn that Alan had never made that particular point before yet I suddenly realised that this was not, in fact, the first time. What was going on? I was neither deaf nor stupid so how come I literally hadn't heard him?

As I reflected I realised that this phenomenon was closely linked to my self-image. Anything that Alan, or anyone else for that matter, might say to me that didn't fit my self-image got filtered out.

Eventually, I came to see that this is one way the psyche shields itself from having to confront something it is not yet ready to. I was only able to hear Alan's point when I was psychologically and emotionally ready.

Lower back pain was not my only experience of pain. I started to experience pain in my left knee, which gradually reached a pitch where I couldn't function properly any more. My Mask insisted that my body and my mind were not connected and, therefore, carried on as usual. My interpretation of what it meant to be "strong" put me under intense pressure.

At home I allowed my pain and my fear free reign. One day when the pain was particularly intense I burst into tears. I sobbed to Jim "what am I going to do! I'll be helpless, disabled, a burden! I'm so scared!" His reply was "Don't be silly". End of story.

His reaction did nothing to reassure me that it was safe to admit to the state I was really in. Unfortunately, pretending that nothing was wrong made me behave erratically, irrationally and inappropriately with my colleagues until, eventually, my supervisor asked me what the hell was going on? I finally broke down and admitted the extent of the pain and how scared and helpless I felt.

I was sent home and went straight to my doctor who over the previous months had made a variety of diagnoses and tried different treatments which made no difference whatsoever. "At this stage, the only thing I can advise you to do is to listen to your body", he concluded.

I sheepishly agreed to stop playing the hero, went home, lay on the sofa with my leg raised and rested for a full week. That was the first time I allowed myself to admit that I couldn't handle the pain any longer.

That break made a real difference and I returned to work in a state of optimism. Now that everybody knew about the pain in my leg, I started using the crutches provided by the hospital. For a while I felt that the self-imposed pressure had lifted.

28

I reach a turning point

However, as the weeks progressed the stressful work situation remained unchanged – my unrealistic expectations, my unwillingness to ask for help, keeping up the façade in front my colleagues continued.

As if that wasn't enough, I changed even more, behaving in ways I thought Team Leaders were supposed to – more formal with my team, which goes against my very nature. As a result, my relationship with my colleagues changed as well, and not for the better.

My relationship with John also changed because my perception of him had altered. Now that he was my Director rather than my friend, I believed I had to act differently. I was more cautious about what I said whilst pretending I knew more than I did. I suspected that he saw right through me and knew that it was all "spin", but I simply couldn't help myself.

To prove I was really useful to have around, I became obsessed with the idea that I had to support the Client Development Department single-handedly. This was an old habit of mine: if I could prove that I could fix, save or rescue, then "they" would need, appreciate and value me. Only then would I be "all right" and somehow "safe".

Finally, John called me into his office and said: "I must admit I made a big mistake taking you away from a job you really enjoyed and were good at, so Anita (my immediate supervisor) will take over all your duties apart from the selling."

My immediate reaction was sheer relief. I wouldn't have to attend those management meetings anymore. I never really fitted in, I had not been making a useful contribution and was wasting my time. Now I could go back to the job I really enjoyed and everything would be all right. But, actually, this change made very little difference. I was still being swallowed up by my old self-destructive habits, beliefs and expectations about how I should be. My professional relationship with John affected our friendship. Even though I went back to my original job I still didn't feel able to tell John how I felt about anything, the way I used to; the way we used to. The previous ease between us was gone.

I also felt uncomfortable telling my team that I was no longer their Team Leader. Although I never detected a hint of it, I started imagining them talking behind my back about how incompetent and useless I'd been and how I deserved to have been cut to size. I retreated within myself.

My colleagues, John, Anita and the others on the team were all incredibly patient. They tried to give me as much support as they could; they told me repeatedly that I didn't need to do it all on my own, that I was part of a team and that I was not alone, but I simply couldn't hear them. The truth was that I didn't believe them. I didn't believe that I could be other than strong and self-sufficient to be acceptable. The idea of exposing my obvious vulnerability terrified me. My fears and habitual thinking habits were louder and more persistent than the efforts of my friends and colleagues to get me to see sense.

Clearly, my Mask was still firmly in place.

John then told me how much I had changed and that I wasn't the person he knew and had asked to join his team. He told me that I had lost my power. I had no idea what he meant by that. I felt confused, as if I were thrashing about, trying not to drown. It made me just try all the harder, doing more of the same since I didn't know what else to do. I was not only well on my way to losing my job but also a dear and loyal friend because, no matter how hard he tried, he just could not reach me.

The turning point came when he finally suggested that perhaps I should become a self-employed consultant again. Those words – "self-employed consultant" – triggered in me the most intense feeling of panic. I felt as if I was drowning in a vortex of terror. It brought back all my old fears of destitution and "cardboard city". It was awful. He suggested I go home early and think about it.

I had told Jim very little of what was going on at work and, if he had noticed my increasingly stressed state, he certainly didn't comment. I didn't tell Jim of my conversation with John when I got back home. I just sat at the living room table staring at the wall. I felt I'd reached rock bottom. It was then that strange things started to happen. The only way I know how to describe it is like pictures flashing through my head, all of them showing me exactly how I was creating my own reality, that is, how I myself was at the root of everything that was happening to me at work.

I suddenly saw how I had been creating the very situation I said I didn't want. I was being needy and dependent, kept asking a lot of unnecessary questions because I believed, wrongly, that it would save time. I kept bothering other people for help with trivial things rather than using my own initiative, I was actually being really irritating and a burden instead of adding value. I was continually acting cheerful when I was feeling anything but that and pretending to be in control, although anyone less in control would be hard to imagine. Trying hard to conceal my feelings and carry on as if it were "business as usual", I was projecting a false image and nobody was taken in. Although they patiently continued to offer help and reassurance I turned them all down assuring everybody I was all right. Inside I felt frightened and defensive and was unable to respond to genuine offers of help.

Earlier on I said how most of my life was governed by fear until fear became a habit. When self-employed I was afraid most of the time because my income was so sporadic that I could never plan. The nature of a freelance way of life is a rollercoaster of feast and famine. Although, looking back at the end of each financial year, the income was always there yet I was never sure where the next project would come from. The spectre of losing my home was always in the forefront of my mind.

And then, when I finally got everything I ever wanted – a job I enjoyed and was good at, a regular income, really nice colleagues, and let's not forget the pension – I actually believed that the fear would go away, except that now I was terrified I would lose it all and, if I did, I was terrified I would lose my home as well.

Perhaps what I was really afraid of was to lose love, to lose my image of myself (that person "I liked to believe I was"), to lose my home, to lose my job. So much fear!

It was only the next day that I finally told Jim that I was afraid I might lose my job.

"Why don't you ask Alan for help?", he suggested. The words that came out of my mouth before I knew it were,

"He's been trying but I wouldn't let him".

It was only when I heard myself say those words that I saw how I was blocking people's attempts to help me. I used two very powerful mechanisms: I would either pretend I was OK because I kept thinking I didn't want to be a "burden", thereby becoming even more of a burden or, what was even more common, I became "confused", that is "I couldn't understand" what people were trying to say to me. But there was more. I suddenly saw how I was holding onto a lot of stuff because of my tendency of wanting to be right which was another facet of my "control-freakery".

Something else I couldn't see at the time was an issue centred around my performance appraisal. My supervisor had set my performance targets for the coming year and, thinking they were totally unreasonable, I refused to sign the form. "She's just being perverse", I told myself, "I just have to get her to see it."

I saw now that I wanted to be right more than I wanted to be happy and at peace.

The next day was probably the most dramatic one in my life. I was scheduled to meet Alan. My regular meetings with him were common knowledge and had John's blessing.

On that day Jon, my colleague, came over to me. "I hope your meeting with Alan works out all right", he said in a tone of voice usually reserved for very young children or very sick people.

"This meeting is just the beginning of a process, nothing more", I replied rather impatiently.

Little did I know.

29

Transformation

The moment everything changed will remain forever etched in my mind.

I was well into my session with Alan and telling him of my experiences over the last two days. Then I stopped. And from somewhere deep inside me I cried out "I don't want to live like this anymore!"

When I look back over all my moments of transformation and healing, that tends to be the point I seem to need to get to in order to allow myself to surrender: My rock bottom place, that place where there's nothing left but to let go of whatever control I pretended I had.

That experience felt so powerful and intense that it was like a mystical Knowing. Now I realise it was even more significant: It was the moment when I finally took responsibility.

In fact, I have come to understand that when I take responsibility by making a conscious choice, any choice, no matter how small or subtle, that's when things can change. I now realise that sometimes I make a choice even when I'm not aware I'm making one.

"I don't want this anymore" is a powerful example of those choices even or perhaps, especially when I don't know what comes next.

I had left the office in a state of emotional darkness. Destitution had come one step closer with the threat of self-employment. Memories of past struggles were jostling for position in my mind – the fear, the uncertainty, the strain, the stress and, especially, the loneliness of struggling on my own. I was going to re-experience it all over again. That thought had nearly paralysed me with terror.

When I returned to the office the following day I was no longer the same person. I felt transformed. My fear had totally disappeared. But it was more than the absence of fear. The space was filled with a deep 'Knowing' that everything would be all right; that I would be all right and that I was going to make it all right. This 'Knowing' is not intellectual; it is a bodily sensation; it is something deep inside me, a 'Knowing' that produced a feeling of lightness, like a weight being lifted from my shoulders. The absence of feeling slightly nauseous which usually signified anxiety was replaced with a light fluttering sensation, like butterfly wings in my tummy which felt like excitement and peace (or was it relief?) all at the same time.

My 'presence' felt tall and self-assured. I walked into the office with a smile on my face and an obvious eagerness to start the day. The contrast between the previous day and that day could not have been more marked. Clearly, it was not the Sue my colleagues had expected to see. I could feel their eyes popping out of their sockets. I smiled to myself. I heard later that even people outside my department were not only commenting about this transformation but making bets that it wouldn't last. It was a topic that lasted a couple of days.

The first thing I did was to go to my immediate supervisor. I had locked horns with her and we were both in entrenched positions, neither one prepared to give in. The question flashed through my mind: 'Do I want to be right or do I want to be happy?' There was no contest. I signed the appraisal form. I also asked that my job status remain unchanged. I did not want to be a self-employed consultant. The request was instantly granted.

I was relieved nobody asked me the obvious question, "What on earth happened to you!?" because I would not have been able to answer it.

I started to really enjoy my job again. I had always enjoyed it but somehow I had got in my own way with my expectations and beliefs about how I should be. Now there was nothing to stop me from regaining that buzz.

I was more proactive which helped me add value and only asked for help when I genuinely needed it. I stopped pretending I knew what I was doing when I didn't and, at the same time, stopped pretending I didn't know things I did. I no longer acted as if I was meant to save the department single-handedly, especially since it didn't need saving and, most important of all, I was genuinely cheerful and having fun again. And when I wasn't feeling cheerful, I didn't hide it anymore.

Of course, on the outside nothing had actually changed, the people were the same, the circumstances, the job with all its pressures were all still the same yet everything had changed because I had changed and, therefore, so had the way I experienced my reality, the world around me. It wasn't just my attitude; my perceptions and interpretations of my circumstances had also undergone a sea change. This affected my reactions and responses to whatever turned up.

Nobody thought it would last but I just couldn't come this close to seeing the very mechanisms I used to create my own life experience and not be changed forever – except, of course, when I revert to old patterns which occasionally does happen.

Something else I have learned from this experience is the extent to which my relationships with other people are shaped by my relationship with myself. Despite my self-image assuring me that I was a nice person, deep down – below the level of my consciousness – I didn't really like myself, I didn't really like that woman called Sue Plumtree. She was the embodiment of falsehood – this was something I sensed only in the subtlest way – and she was also a woman I didn't really trust because 'she' would let me down and cause me to betray and sabotage myself. I only understood this dimly and had no idea what to do about it.

That experience taught me something else I hadn't understood. Change is a process with many insights and understandings along the way and this was when my poor health came to my rescue yet again. Poor health and even pain need not necessarily be only a cause of suffering; it can also be a powerful teacher.

30

How my relationship with others really work

Because I had lived an empty and lonely life for so long I was always yearning for friendships to alleviate that emptiness and loneliness. The only way I knew how to make friends was at a superficial level. Emotional honesty, integrity and authenticity played no part.

I remember the very moment when my journey towards truth and integrity actually started.

In 1997 I enrolled on a ten week introductory course in Psychosynthesis. Simply put, the aim of Psychosynthesis is to achieve a coming together of the various parts of an individual's personality into a more cohesive self, including the inner world which also takes account of the soul.

I was sitting on the train, reading the required chapter and choosing from a list of activities as part of my homework. Going down the list, my eyes alighted on "do something you have never done before". Instantly a thought formed in my mind that startled me out of my seat: "Tell the truth".

I had never regarded myself as an untruthful person, at least no better or worse than the next one so I found that thought unsettling. True to form, I set it aside because I had no idea what it was all about nor what to do with the invitation.

As it happened, I was on my way to one of my regular sessions with Alan and I was wrestling with a "minor" feeling of resentment and feeling trapped. The issue was that in one of the groups I had joined participants had been paired off as support partners for each other. It was my turn to make the phone call to my support partner that week and I was dreading it.

I met Alan and within minutes I was well into my whingeing session.

"He's so boring!", I complained, "he goes on and on about the most trivial things in the most minute detail!".

I went on in this vein a little while longer. Eventually, Alan made a simple comment.

"Tell the truth", he said. I felt as if I had been punched in the stomach. First I felt the shock of seeing the connection, then I felt absolutely aghast.

"I can't do that!", I exclaimed, "Friends are supposed to listen to one another. I can't not listen, it would be selfish!" (the sub-text of which was "I don't want him to think I'm selfish").

Alan explained, "But you're not listening so you would not be a true friend and you're feeling resentful. Calling him and pretending to listen while you're feeling resentful and unable to listen is not being a friend." I couldn't think of anything to say.

The very next day I phoned my support partner and said something along the lines that this was not a good time for me to talk and I would not be able to listen to him properly. I don't remember the precise words I used but I do remember the terror. I don't think the word 'terror' in this context is too excessive a word for what I felt. Fear of hurting, fear of offending, fear of rejection, fear of abandonment, fear of being seen as selfish and a bad friend – all rolled into one. Yet I did make that call and I did manage to get the words out. After I had hung up, I sat there, staring at the phone and going over the conversation I'd just had.

"Thank you for being honest with me", he'd said, "I totally understand. Let's talk some other time."

I could hardly believe it, after all the agonies I had put myself through.

Such a seemingly prosaic and trivial incident marked the beginning of a journey which continues to take me deeper and deeper into what it means to be truthful.

I saw that being truthful involves first and foremost being truthful with myself: what I really feel, what is really true for me, what I really need, what really works for me and what really does not. And then – and only then, ideally, to express it to the person concerned. I say 'ideally' because that isn't always possible yet I do believe that, where humanly possible, I need to tell the person concerned.

The more I started to pay attention – both to myself and others – the more I began to see that qualities which may in themselves be admirable and noble can actually be abused and misused, for example, loyalty and unconditional support. Here's an example:

A while back I met Jane, an old acquaintance, whom I hadn't seen in a long time. We went down "memory lane" for a while along the lines of "have you heard from 'x'?" and "what happened to 'y'?". In the course of our conversation the name of a common acquaintance came up from whom I had parted several years previously in very painful circumstances.

I'd felt extremely hurt at the time but, by now, the pain had long gone. What struck me, however, was how Jane spat all kinds of insults against this ex-acquaintance probably in the mistaken belief that demonising someone who had hurt "her" friend was demonstrating solidarity and support. I admit I used to do the same. This is not a good thing to do (allowing others to demonise someone) because it makes me into "an innocent bystander" or victim in the story when reality is a whole lot more complex. It causes me to blame another person – which I did at great length at the time – or let someone else do so on my behalf which, I admit, used to make me feel loved and supported. It also made it easy for me to avoid taking responsibility for my part in the situation.

This next example is particularly important for me because it encompasses a wide range of issues, each fundamental in its own right, such as listening to myself, expectations, taking responsibility. This also includes the dynamics of relationships in terms of what comes first, the chicken or the egg, or, put another way, who needs to change first, "them" or me in order for a relationship to change.

In 1981 I had made a promise to Papi that, in exchange for leaving Gloucester to move in with Jim again, I would phone every single day. This I did, religiously, for the next nineteen years, even after he died in 1988.

From a purely practical perspective, phoning every day was possible when I was self-employed and working from home. But, in 1999, when I started working full time in London and commuting every day, I would be very tired by the time I got home in the evening. There was often a subtle niggly feeling in the region of my stomach, sitting on the train on my way back and thinking 'I still have to phone Mami' and pretend everything is OK (even when things weren't). Otherwise I'd have to go into long explanations and I just couldn't face it. I always told myself that the calls would usually be short, and, after all, she's "a little old lady" and it wasn't such a big deal anyway. I probably would still be calling every day with a faint but ever-growing feeling of resentment gnawing at me, unable to let go of my self-expectation that calling one's little old Mum every day is what "good" daughters do.

It was Alan who finally brought up the subject. It was during one of our sessions that he unexpectedly asked, "Are you still calling your Mum every day?" I was taken totally off-guard. With Alan there is no such thing as an innocuous question.

"Yes", I replied, cautiously, wondering where this was going.

"And how do you feel about it?", he continued.

I suddenly felt as if I'd been found out. Here was yet another place I didn't want to visit but now I had no choice.

"Trapped", I said, "and resentful".

I stopped. I couldn't believe what I was saying. Alan had actually noticed my growing feeling of resentment combined with my habit of going into denial whenever I didn't want to face anything challenging. He clearly felt it was time to bring it out into the open.

Once we got past my denial I came up against yet another obstacle to being authentic: fear. No, not fear, terror. Yes, I notice I use the word 'terror' a lot. However, I'm staying with this word because it highlights the extent to which I would convert feelings such as anxiety and fear into terror as a way to oppress myself and paralyse myself into a stand-still. Fear is much more manageable than terror.

So, just thinking about telling my "little old Mami" that I didn't want to continue calling her every day filled me with terror -any kind of confrontation carried with it the threat of abandonment. I just "knew" she would disown me, never speak to me again, accuse me of not loving her and never having done so and on and on. And on. I also "knew" that I just wouldn't be able to handle this onslaught because, on top of everything else, the guilt would eat me up.

Alan then brought up the term 'non-love' and it was then that I suddenly saw with total clarity for the first time how this non-love manifested itself in the context of my relationship with Mami. I saw that if she tried to manipulate me (one of her habits) into feeling guilty (one of my habitual responses to her manipulation) then this would not be love – it would be non-love.

Although this was a hugely important insight, it took several sessions with Alan to explore my reluctance and anxiety. My habitual beliefs about how I should be as a daughter, my perceptions of Mami as a "little old lady" totally dependent on my one phone call per day made me feel intensely selfish and, of course, 'selfish' was not a part of my self image.

Eventually I felt strong and secure within myself, especially now that I had a firm grasp of what 'non-love' actually feels like. It is a feeling I had been familiar with for what seemed forever but I'd had no words to describe it. Now that it had been named, I knew how to deal with it when it came up – if it came up.

I thought a lot about this and was absolutely clear about what I wanted to say and why. The fear had left me. I knew this was something I could not say over the phone; I had to do it face-to-face so I waited until our next visit.

Jim knew what I was planning to do and he disapproved because 'it's only one call and, after all, she's a little old lady.' I had not only brainwashed myself; I had brainwashed him too.

So, after lunch, Jim made himself scarce and, after delaying the evil moment for as long as I could until it was nearly time to leave I finally took my courage in my two hands and told her.

"I have something I need to say to you. I love you very much but I really don't want to call you every day anymore." To my amazement, she took it really well.

"That's good!", she replied, "It's often inconvenient for me to wait by the phone."

I was amazed at her response. I was delighted it had gone so well, much better than I had hoped, but also felt a bit miffed that it had been so easy. I had sort of hoped for an opportunity to stand up to her somewhat more heroically.

This hope was soon realised, however. She started deploying various non-loving tactics which I now could recognise as such. She would accuse me of not caring about her and that a brief phone call wasn't a lot to ask for and so on. For the first time in my life, I did not let myself get emotionally sucked into the murky brew of expectations – hers of me and mine of myself, her attempts at manipulating me and the inevitable feelings of guilt, resentment and helplessness.

This was new territory for both of us. I needed to be patient and repeatedly explain that the reason I didn't want to call her every day was not because I didn't love her but because I was feeling resentful and that was getting in the way of my genuine love for her.

The other thing she needed to hear, also over and over again, was that, when we spoke on the phone, I wanted it to be because we really wanted to talk with each other and not a duty to get over and done with as quickly as possible.

Over the next few weeks she began to experience for herself that, when we spent "quality" time together as opposed to our previous perfunctory exchanges, she would feel more heard and more loved than before. Our relationship changed into one that is now strong, mature and genuinely loving.

What I learned was that my relationship with Mami changed because I first changed the way I perceived myself and how I expected myself to be. This incident showed me that people treat me at my own valuation of myself. This whole episode became a huge milestone for me.

Gradually, I learned to trust myself instead of always relying on other people's opinions. After all, I'm the one who's ultimately responsible for my own choices even when I choose to follow someone else's advice. I might as well follow my own judgment since, at the end of the day, I can only grow by learning from my mistakes.

I started wondering about the relationship between trusting my own judgement and liking myself. Now that I had Alan in my life the process of learning to like myself began to take on a whole new meaning.

He first encouraged me to start noticing my inner dialogue, that is, what I tell myself and the tone I use when talking to myself. For example, am I impatient with myself? Am I being self-critical and do I beat myself up? Do I pay attention to what's important to me? Do I even know what is important to me? Do I trust myself? And what does it mean to trust myself?

"To start making friends with yourself it is necessary", Alan explained, "that you make friends with all of yourself – both the positive and the negative qualities that remain hidden from view. This is called the Shadow, which is a Jungian term. It refers to qualities that you regard as fearsome and unacceptable."

I had never looked at any of my dark aspects – simply because it was obvious that I had no Shadow side. I was a nice person, nothing more, nothing less.

I had spent most of my adult life nurturing my False Self in order to be liked and loved, developing all those qualities that my parents had drummed into me were necessary for my survival – being charming, helpful, supportive, generous, loyal, interested in others and undemanding. It was a Mask that was beginning to outgrow any use it might have had.

Meanwhile, my Shadow – that part of me I could under no circumstances accept on pain of being rejected or abandoned – continued to drive and sabotage me.

Over time Alan kept explaining that confronting and integrating my Shadow was essential for the sake of my health and my humanity. The fact was that I had ignored both my Shadow and the False Self, which I believed was the real me. The results, as evidenced by the life I was living, were impossible to ignore.

➢ I was living a precarious financial reality, compounded by spending beyond my means. I did what I believed was necessary to look attractive, since I assumed that was the key to being accepted, even loved. I believed that looking attractive confirmed or even enhanced my worth.

My False Self whispered in my ear that everything I was doing to look good was essential to my survival – despite having no financial stability. This made me intensely vulnerable without my being aware of it.

➢ In my relationships I tended to run Jim down and present myself as a victim. I believed (as far as I was aware I was doing it) that this approach would get me sympathy and support.

My False Self encouraged me by whispering in my ear that eliciting compassion and understanding was simply another way to be loved.

➤ I took a lover to find the love and attention I was missing in my marriage. I justified it to myself as having a lot of love to give without realising that, with affairs, come lying and cheating.

My False Self whispered in my ear that, since Jim didn't meet my needs, it was alright to try and meet them elsewhere.

➤ When I finally did get a job that I enjoyed and was good at I nearly lost it by choosing to be right instead of happy.

My False Self whispered in my ear that being right was essential to my survival.

Alan explained all this over many sessions until I finally understood it deep down in my body. My unacknowledged and un-integrated Shadow drove me to make choices and decisions from the undergrowth of my subconscious that were against the interests of what I now define as my material, emotional, psychological and spiritual values.

Of course I knew I had some weaknesses. Who doesn't? I didn't mind admitting that, for example, I was a bit untidy, perhaps even very untidy, certainly undomesticated. I also had to accept that I sometimes tended to become a little over-enthusiastic when I was with somebody, for example, I would tend to finish their sentences. I knew I shouldn't but I just wanted them to know how much I understood where they were coming from. But, really, that's all I could think of.

However, I couldn't get away from the fact that "doing nice" made me neither happy, nor created authentic relationships. My life was not fulfilling and meaningful. I was no longer prepared to live an empty and lonely life and so in the end, I did reach the point where I became willing to take responsibility. By then, the only way forward was for me to take a peek at that so-called Shadow of mine.

The first thing I noticed was how I had dealt with those unacceptable characteristics until then. I would spot the same faults in others and be so outraged that my strong feelings of revulsion made me extremely judgmental. Alternatively, I simply denied those traits within myself.

The task of uncovering who I really was – the whole of me, not just the bits and pieces I liked best – enabled me to take a major step in my journey towards liking myself. The journey was as vital as the end goal.

I am aware that there are more depths for me to uncover, not only the dark aspects but also their opposite. For example: lying and cheating at one end and truth and integrity at the other; greedy and selfish versus generous and thoughtful, reckless and thoughtless at one extreme and sensitive and tactful at the other.

At times it's as if I were a jigsaw puzzle where the picture is gradually beginning to emerge.

The self-deception that I abandoned before all the others was being nice all the time. I now like to think that I am truthful and honest, and that I act with integrity at all times. Except, of course (and this is hard for me to face up to) when there's something in it for me. I also "like to think" that I'm honest and transparent. 'Hypocritical', for example, is not an adjective that I find easy to accept about myself.

I had to confront this aspect when I recognised that the time had come for an old friendship to end. This couple and I had known each other for many years. In fact, I had been friends with each of them separately and had introduced them to each other. Recently I noticed they were not comfortable with the new "me".

Previously, I had deceived myself about many things, in particular about my marriage. I would complain about Jim on one occasion, and on another I would go on about how wonderful he was, a pattern that had become predictable and probably more than a little tiresome. Now I had developed a new clarity and inner strength with which they were unfamiliar.

I remember one particular occasion when I met her.

"It's wonderful the way Jim accepts you", she observed.

"To be accepted", I replied, "you need to be known."

She looked startled. "I never thought of it like that", she said.

I thought I detected a faint feeling of discomfort and wondered about the state of her own relationship.

As I continued to change I began to notice that her responses had become lukewarm and polite, and I had less and less to say to her. Then she told me they were having a house clear-out. They had so many beautiful things that I had admired over the years, I decided to postpone letting the relationship fizzle out until I saw what they were getting rid of in case there was something I might want. Clearly a knee-jerk reaction because the style in which they had decorated their home was far removed from ours and, in any case, we didn't even have the space. Despite this, I decided to postpone my decision and keep my options open, just in case. Fortunately, it didn't take me long to come to my senses.

Keeping my options open in a situation that brought me nothing of genuine worth was a life-long habit. I hated potentially missing out on something – anything. But I came to see that, by doing so, I was losing more than I was gaining. I was losing my self-respect.

This process of confronting and integrating my Shadow has, at times, felt overwhelming. One approach that helped was to examine something equally powerful and more manageable – looking into what love and non-love actually mean in the context of my own life.

31

Love and non-love

I have already mentioned how powerful the impact was when I first came across the term 'non-love' in the context of my relationship with Mami.

Also how I was only able to take off my Mask gradually, by focusing on one aspect of my life at a time. The concept of 'non-love' was the exception. I took the ball and ran with it in all parts of my life.

Shocking things emerged: I discovered that I believed myself to be unworthy of love. The realisation struck my consciousness when I thought about what my relationships felt like – and this is where 'non-love' shed a light: I tended to feel unheard and unimportant to the other person, I resorted to collusion so as to be loved, encouraging others people to act in ways that made me feel manipulated. Fearful that they would turn against me, I submerged my own wants and needs, and even isolated myself when I needed others most, in the belief that exposing my vulnerability would turn me into a burden.

Other ways I tried to be worthy of love were to make myself indispensable. I offered unwanted advice, tried to fix and rescue the people I cared about to get them to need me and, therefore, depend on me. That would make me necessary to them and that, I believed, was love.

Another misconception about love was that it was only really related to romantic and sexual relationships. Of course, I always knew that parents love their children, that children love their parents and that people love their friends and their pets. But, to me, "real" love was mostly of the romantic variety. In this context, I had another belief, too, which was that only sentimentality, romance and tenderness equalled love.

What I didn't understand was that love is so much, much more. It starts with self-love or, a term I prefer, by making friends with oneself. It means knowing what really matters and feeling free to express it; listening to my own needs rather than putting other people first at my own expense and then resenting them for it; making choices that positively affect my physical, emotional and spiritual well-being and peace of mind; establishing personal boundaries about what is and is not acceptable; taking responsibility for my life and recognising the extent to which I am its creator, instead of blaming others or declaring life to be unfair; letting myself feel what I really do feel, rather than what other people say I should feel; standing up for what I believe is right and true, even when it is unpopular; more than anything, feeling I am OK even when I fall short of my own or somebody else's expectations.

Love means gratitude for everything that happens to me, even if I don't like it at the time and honouring that gift by trying to learn from its message. Love is also knowing this may take time, assuming I learn at all. And that's OK too. And still, this is a very narrow definition.

However, I am still gripped by limited and limiting beliefs about love that have been inculcated in me by my parents, by society, even by religious dogma: That for me, as a woman, to be loved (mostly sexually and romantically), I have to be beautiful (as defined by standards set by the media) and, especially, that I have to behave a certain way to be worthy of love. Every one of us fills in the gap created by this vague term "a certain way" themselves. I've filled it in with "charming, agreeable, loyal, helpful, supportive, cheerful", and so on. Others may fill it in differently.

I have noticed how being true to myself has affected my relationships. For instance as in 2001, when I had an interesting experience.

Lillian – I used to call her 'a friend' (I called everybody whom I knew more than casually a 'friend') – and I had known each other for many years. Recently it struck me that our telephone conversations or meetings could best be described as non-communications; full of empty pap and non-events. I wanted to drop this empty "friendship" so I stopped calling her hoping she would get the message and the relationship would fizzle out. But she would always call. I finally decided that I had to behave honestly and then either the relationship would become closer or end altogether. So, whenever we talked I would be as true as I knew how, particularly when we were in "catching-up" mode, saying not only how well everything was going in my life but also where I was struggling. I had never been this honest with her before.

One day she invited Jim and me for lunch in her new flat. My marriage was facing great challenges at the time. I was in turbulence, feeling despair, sadness and fear, and I really needed to talk but, even when we were alone in the kitchen, she side-stepped all my attempts to confide in her.

I remember feeling awful by the time we got home. I decided to call her the next day and tell her how I was feeling, not about my marriage, but about my relationship with her. This sounds like I made a straight-forward decision. Nothing could be further from the truth. I was terrified of being so direct and truthful, something completely new to me. Indeed, truth, emotional exposure and vulnerability were synonymous with the fear of rejection.

Paradoxically, even the worst case scenario, ending the relationship, would be what I had wanted all along!

My heart pounding, I called her. I bought myself some time by going through the social formalities. Eventually, I couldn't avoid the real purpose of my phone call any longer. I took a deep breath and said, "There's something I need to tell you. I wanted to confide in you about what's really been going on in my life. Although I did try you didn't give me the opportunity and I'm now feeling distanced from you."

She said all the right things. She exclaimed how upset she was to hear me say that, how she had felt inhibited talking about things because Jim was sitting in the other room and she promised that we would meet for lunch and open our hearts to each other as soon as she returned from her trip abroad. That was the last time I heard from her.

Not all examples have such a clear-cut outcome. Here is another one, illustrating how I came to see that even good intentions – when combined with non-love – can be important and disturbing lessons.

I was on a two day assignment for the business school where I lectured. For the first time I was to be responsible for a workshop in which I had previously only acted as an assistant. I had been allocated my own assistant for the first of the two days. He happened to be black and, because he arrived late, there was no time to share out the sessions of the day. When I tried to do so in the morning break, he told me: "You're on your own; I'm only here because I was told to be" and refused to step in when I was struggling.

The following day I was scheduled to work with someone with whom I had worked before. The experience of that first day had left me shocked and deeply angry, so much so that I couldn't stop talking about it. It finally dawned on me that this was definitely not the right way of handling my feelings. I knew that I needed to talk with that man face-to-face.

This was a momentous decision. All my life my inclination had been to avoid any kind of confrontation, preferring instead to vent my frustration and anger by telling others about a particular incident – and this was no exception. So the mere fact that I was sitting there face-to-face with this man was both a source of pride and deep anxiety.

I had spent a lot of time thinking about how I was to open the conversation and finally came up with "I needed you to know that I have no intention of ever working with you again, because I can't trust you to be there for me when I need you. Is there anything you'd like to say about it?".

Of the whole conversation what struck me most is that his side of the story was exclusively related to his experience as a black teacher at that College. I explained to him that the incident on that particular day had nothing to do with colour, but with him and me as colleagues. It soon became clear that he was either unable or unwilling to hear me. He kept talking about how he was being discriminated against because he was black and ignored everything I was saying until, finally, completely exasperated, I exclaimed, "You're doing to me what you're telling me others are doing to you!" but it made no difference and the end of the conversation was, for me at least, unsatisfactory. I felt unheard and so, I suspect, did he.

What has this example to do with non-love? Here is the connection.

I'm presenting myself as the "good guy" in this story: the one who was hard done by, who tried to be reasonable and approachable and he let me down in every conceivable way. And yet, this tendency to present myself in a positive light (to myself as well as to the person I'm telling the story to) has an important consequence, namely that the other person becomes, by implication, the "bad guy" and that is non-loving.

If I'm the "good guy" then it becomes much easier to see the other person as lacking in understanding, insight, empathy, self-awareness and so on, that is, the complete "opposite" of me and the result is separation between us. I find this insight extremely disturbing, so it is very important for me to watch my step. I wonder if, had I been less self-righteous, we might have connected better.

One assertion I have often come across is that love is unconditional and that this is the difference between love and need. Love needs nothing, so they say, yet I did have needs that I wanted to have met, particularly by Jim.

However hard it was for me to start expressing my true feelings to Lillian, the woman in the first example, and feeling terrified of exposing myself despite the fact that I didn't care whether she stayed in my life or not, it was even harder to make myself emotionally vulnerable to Jim.

When I did, he would either say nothing, shrug helplessly, look perplexed or give a nervous laugh. My initial reaction when faced with his lack of response was to withdraw. It was such a painful experience I really felt I couldn't handle it. And then I realised something fundamental. Being authentic is something I am for my own sake, not for anybody else. I don't make myself emotionally vulnerable to get a specific response or result however much I would like one (preferably one that goes my way) but because this is who I am or, at least, whom I aim to become.

Recognising non-love for what it is – mostly an expression of fear – has become incredibly useful in helping me identify the many ways in which I act in non-loving ways, whether towards others or towards myself (especially towards myself). There were many ways in which I allowed others to act in non-loving ways towards me because I had never set boundaries about what is or is not acceptable to me. I now know that, to be able to set clear boundaries, I really need to truly like myself, to regard myself as worthy of saying "No, this is not acceptable".

I've also come to see that I'd misguidedly regarded many of my own non-loving behaviours as loving ones, for example, when I'd act in self-sacrificing ways at my own expense. Continuing to call my Mum despite my feelings of resentment is a case in point; shielding Jim from life's challenges and carrying all kinds of burdens on my own without sharing them with him or anybody else for that matter is another.

Influenced by seeing Mami always putting Papi first, I assumed that putting others first is a powerful way of expressing my love. Looking after myself and my own needs and wants was, therefore, selfish and, since all I ever wanted was to be seen as a generous and loving person, I ended up completely out of touch with what I wanted and needed. What I missed at the time, though, was that, by always putting herself last Mami felt unappreciated and resentful and would make her resentment clear.

I remember one particular example. Jim and I went to visit them in Buenos Aires in 1968 to celebrate Papi's 60th birthday. During our stay, Mami decided to make curtains for our new home in the States. It turned out to be a mammoth task that took much longer than she'd expected and which meant that Jim, Papi and I would go out by ourselves, leaving her behind. We kept asking her to join us but she refused saying she had these curtains to finish and sounding extremely resentful and hard done by. And woe betide us if we didn't repeatedly appreciate her efforts – which we did, at every opportunity.

When I first came across the term 'non-love' I made the connection that the other side of love is not hate or indifference – it is non-love and, over time, I have uncovered many of the ways in which I used to express non-love. One of my insights has been that non-love is particularly insidious when superficially the issue appears to be minor one.

I learned about how I expressed (or experienced) non-love: I acted non-lovingly towards myself when I pretended to be what I wasn't, when I denied the so-called unacceptable aspects of myself and was willing to deny another person's humanity by pretending they were just sweetness and light. I also acted non-lovingly towards myself by failing to listen to my needs or my intuition, I let myself down and acted without integrity.

I cannot repeat often enough that I have deceived, colluded and manipulated others without seeing the truth. I never meant any harm. I simply never gave it a thought. Ducking and weaving through life, I was merely intent on surviving. As a consequence, I have also often been at the receiving end of non-love.

A typical example was my friendship with Meg, whom I would sometimes meet for a meal. Gradually I noticed that, whenever we spent time together, I felt as if I had to earn her approval. Afterwards I experienced a sense of worthlessness. She had developed a habit of blanking out unwelcome information. This happened every time I tried to tell her how I felt. She would not respond to the point I made but, instead, she would make light of it by saying in a jokey tone of voice "I know when I'm not wanted!"

The very thought of hurting or offending anyone made me feel intensely guilty so just being honest about my feelings felt risky. The message of never ever hurting anybody's feelings had been drummed into me since childhood and so I'd retreat saying "No, no! You got me all wrong, I really want you!" or words to that effect. We would kiss and make up, leaving everything unchanged – until the next time.

I finally broke free of her during a telephone conversation that sounded eerily familiar. The key difference this time being that, in anticipation of her phone call, I had propped up a piece of paper in front of me where I'd written 'manipulative'.

The other, far more significant, difference was that I had decided to be pro-active and break off the relationship. My inclination until then had always been to let relationships "fizzle out", so this was a huge decision for me.

The telephone conversation opened with the introductory niceties. Then I said, "Look, I've been thinking a lot about this. I've noticed that when I'm with you I feel inadequate and not at all good about myself. I really don't want to feel like that anymore so I'd rather we don't meet up again." There was a silence, a very long silence. Then, "Oh, all right, I know when I'm not wanted!" This time, instead of my habitual guilt-laden reaction I looked at my little piece of paper propped in front of me and said – "Thank you." And hung up.

I sat there, staring at the phone for a long time unable to believe what I'd just done.

Such mixed feelings of guilt, anxiety, a sense of relief (a huge sense of relief!), pride, even disbelief that I had actually seen this through.

I have discovered even more ways where I have been non-loving towards myself. A really bad one was where I blocked myself from receiving love. I could barely believe I would do this to myself. Blocking love happens when I present the 'I can handle it', façade; 'I don't need any help, thank you very much', 'no, really, I'm fine, thank you' are all variations of the same theme. The idea of emotional exposure was anathema to me. These were the very mechanisms which kept people at a distance blocking out any possibility of love.

Tolerating behaviours that for one reason or another didn't feel right to me (fear of rocking the boat springs to mind) was also non-loving. I now know in a way I didn't know before that it is non-loving – both to myself and to the other person – to let anyone, whoever they may be, get away with inappropriate behaviour, be it thoughtlessness, lack of care, disrespect, manipulation and all other non-loving acts that people have displayed towards me over the decades, sometimes in the name of love.

I have learnt to like myself, trust myself, be true to myself and accept all of myself by a lengthy process of baby steps and insights, learning and healing, bringing with it transformation along the way.

Meanwhile, I had begun to wonder about what I would describe Jim's passive resistance; the things he would say and do – or more hurtful and upsetting, fail to say and do. For example, he never addressed me by my name or nickname. When I was upstairs, instead of calling my name to get my attention, he would just start talking until it penetrated my awareness. Then I'd peer down and ask "Did you say something?". Once I'd noticed I felt very upset and decided that, if he wanted to talk to me, he'd have to come upstairs but I never felt able to see it through. I hated the idea that he might feel ignored.

Very gradually I came to the conclusion that he must harbour some deep resentments towards me. Was it because he had needs I wasn't meeting? Did he feel threatened and vulnerable watching me change before his very eyes? What was it?

I asked him what was missing for him, was there something he wanted or needed from me he wasn't getting? But, despite my repeated efforts, he always denied that anything was wrong.

Then, eventually, I realised that what I took to be passive resistance was more. Here's an example. If there's one thing I really hate, it is last minute rushing and feeling stressed out. That's why I plan things carefully to make sure there's plenty of time – to get to the airport, catch a bus, get to the theatre or cinema. Jim was the complete opposite, always waiting until the last minute. In itself this is nothing special, but he would invariably "mislay" his keys or credit card, rushing helplessly around wailing "I can't understand it! It doesn't make sense!" while my stress levels are going through the roof. This was a regular occurrence but I especially remember one particular occasion.

In 2000 I was awarded the Certificate in Higher Education and there was to be a ceremony at the Royal Festival Hall, complete with gown and cap, where someone high up in the Westminster Business School's hierarchy was to hand us our certificates. We had to go onto the podium, shake hands and receive the paper.

I had never been part of anything like this before. It was, therefore, a hugely special occasion for me.

I had arranged to take a half day off work. The ceremony was scheduled to start at 2:00 and Jim was to collect me at 12:00. With the Royal Festival Hall barely 20 minutes away it also gave us plenty of time for a celebratory meal.

Jim arrived 45 minutes late by which time we had to dash to get there, have a rushed bite to eat, my stomach tight with anxiety, anger and hurt. I remember sitting at the table and looking at the other families, relaxed and smiling, clearly proud of their sons, daughters and siblings. How I envied them.

I had always believed that Jim was merely being disorganised or forgetful until one particular holiday in 2002.

We were in Estepona, a small holiday resort in Andalucia. This was a place I loved and I particularly enjoyed going to the beach and lazing in the sunshine. It was a bus ride away from town and there was only one bus an hour.

Setting up on the beach wasn't just a question of laying down a towel. It required putting up the windbreaker, the sun brolly and surrounding ourselves with a variety of gear, all intended to create comfort and protection from the sharp breeze. It also took at least half hour to take it all down, fold it and pack it away. Then we would climb up the steep embankment to street level and a short walk to the bus stop.

On one particular occasion, having alerted Jim that time was drawing near when we would have to start dismantling the gear and him delaying and delaying for no apparent reason I was suddenly struck with the thought that he was deliberately dragging his feet to wind me up.

All the previous similar occasions over past years flashed through my mind. I suddenly saw with shocking clarity that he wasn't absent minded or distracted as I had always believed. They were gestures calculated to annoy me. When I challenged him he looked sheepish and started getting ready straight away.

I tried to set this insight aside for the remainder of the holiday, but I felt devastated. Did he even like me, I wondered. One thing was clear: he had resentments that ran deep but, since he kept assuring me that everything was just fine there was nothing else I could do.

When Alan and I were trying to work out why I was feeling so sad all those years ago I remember being struck by one of the questions. He had asked me whether I had any relationships in my life that caused me hurt and pain. My reply was "no". Afterwards, I reflected on this, but still came to the same conclusion.

The twelve months that followed this observation clearly showed the extent of my self-deception. But the answer is not obvious. It wasn't just Jim who hurt me, I had hurt myself by staying and now, I have finally arrived at this critical stage when I know I can no longer remain in my marriage. I can now cry out: "I don't want this for myself anymore!"

Conclusions

Probably the most painful part of my journey has been coming to understand the extent to which I myself contributed to the creation of my life so far. I have also come to accept that I cannot carry a relationship single-handedly and, while I have changed and learned and grown, Jim hasn't. Despite all my efforts, he wasn't prepared to meet me half-way and this is why I have reached this stage. I feel overwhelmed with sadness. I wish it hadn't come to this.

BOOK II

MY LIFE WITHOUT MY MASK

32

I separate from Jim –
pages from my journal

It is now February 2003 and all I can say is 'thank God for my little office where I can sit and write'.

About two months ago I wrestled with the question "Am I staying with Jim because I love him or because I'm afraid of being alone?" I found it impossible to answer. I looked at various aspects of my relationship with him. I asked myself, "Does he stop me from doing the things that interest me?" The answer was "No, he doesn't". Does he stop me from meeting my friends? Again I answered, "no". Do I find it difficult to be in his company? "No, we do have good times together." Do I mind that I cannot share with him what matters to me? The answer to that is "yes, I do. But I do have friends I can confide in." The conclusion I came to then was that I simply couldn't find it in me to leave him.

I have also reached what I believe to be the final version of this book. It is a labour of love. Alan suggested it was time I test it with a few anonymous readers. Together we developed a feedback form and I handed my manuscript over to him. This is the first time I have given it to strangers to read. I'm feeling really anxious. How will they react? How will it impact on them? I have decided to set the whole thing aside and get on with other things until the forms are sent back.

It's only been two months since I decided to stay with Jim and that was supposed to be the end of the matter.

I thought I'd stopped my self-destructive behaviours, that I stopped having expectations about my marriage, that I really accepted Jim for who and how he was, that I stopped deceiving myself, that I stopped pretending I was feeling one thing when I was feeling another. I can't believe that I still feel fearful. That upsets me most of all. So the last two months have been very strange. At first I had a sense of completion and that my understanding of where I was in my marriage to Jim reflected that. All the arguments that made me stay with him kept running in my head over and over again, especially since I believed that they were based on what I felt to be true.

Firstly, I feel I'm in "waiting" mode because I still haven't received any feedback from Alan's readers. Apart from Alan and my Mum, no one has seen it, so my perception about any meaning my book might have for potential readers is limited.

I'm also feeling that I've reached the end of my journey and I don't know what comes next. I keep functioning but my heart isn't in it.

About four weeks ago, after walking around weighed down by a feeling of numbness I finally felt able to allow my sadness free expression, a sadness which I had been holding in tightly and, as always, I was surprised at its intensity.

I had genuinely hoped to have reached a place of acceptance about my marriage, and I truly believed that that would be enough.

I remembered a quote from Caroline Myss' 'Anatomy of the Spirit' where she says, "Try as we will, we cannot forever "visit" truth and then return to illusion. At some point the process of change itself moves us forward" – these words are now proving to be true.

I knew I had shed my pretences and denials and had also come to accept that feeling sad occasionally is OK. I decided that the way I was going to deal with the emptiness in my marriage was to pour all my energy and passion into my book. Writing the book would enable me to express myself in a way I have been unable to do within my marriage.

But I have to realise I set myself aside – after everything I have learned, after everything I know – and focused all my energies on the world around me, wrongly believing that was enough.

Yesterday I suddenly noticed, to my shock, that I was deep into my habitual belief of "hopelessness" and "impotence": this is how it is and there's nothing I can do about it. This time, though, given that I'm not prepared to leave Jim, these beliefs seem very real. I feel trapped. I know I have painted myself into a corner and I don't know how to get myself out. Even worse is my feeling that all I learned and expressed in my book is coming back to mock me. All I know about truth, integrity, love and non-love (especially non-love) yet, in this most fundamental part of my life – my marriage – I still feel unable to act on what I know. My book now feels like a lie.

When Alan handed me the feedback notes I couldn't wait to start reading them. I read them on the train home and it was then that I realised the truth. The comments were everything I had hoped for and more. One reader had recognised the intention of my book. She saw many aspects of me in herself; she recognised many of my own fears and deceptions and she fully empathised with me. I could see that she was rooting for me. I couldn't have asked for more. Yet it was my reaction that threw me. It was as if none of it touched me. It wasn't that her feedback didn't matter; it was as if there were a glass wall between myself and what for so long I had thought I wanted the most – and now here it was and it didn't touch me.

That's when I suddenly realised that even this book, on which I have focused all my energies and, yes, love over the last four years sits outside of me. What I have written and who I really am right now simply doesn't match up.

Even if my book were to become a runaway success, it wouldn't alleviate the emptiness and loneliness within my marriage. Thinking back to all the reasons I told myself for staying with Jim, they just sound like hollow excuses.

This habit of mine of compartmentalising myself wasn't working anymore. I now have nowhere to hide because I have become a whole person. I also remembered

– again – that I am the common denominator in my life, and that my life, my reality, does not happen outside of me but within. It actually starts and ends with me.

I had always believed that the life I led outside of my marriage – my relationships, my book, my job, my continued learning and growing, all my new experiences which are deeply important and fulfilling – would be enough and now I see that they're not. They cannot fill the empty space.

It is clear to me that I can't run away anymore although, right now, I don't know what "not running away anymore" actually entails. The mere thought that I might "stop running" brings up a nameless terror in me. So, for the last few weeks I've been alternating between sadness and self-pity; doing what I do best, painting myself into a corner.

I know that it's important for me to honour all my feelings, especially the so-called negative ones because I can learn so much from them – if I let myself. I know this to be true because that is my experience. But it's beginning to dawn on me that the point of feelings is not only to experience them but, once their true cause has been identified, to do something about it – and that's precisely what I feel unable to do, certainly not with the choices I'm giving myself.

I have reflected on why I feel so trapped and I've come up with four key reasons:

1. I feel real affection and tenderness for Jim. I know he loves me in his own way and I often enjoy spending time with him.

2. 37 years of marriage is a very long time and not something I'm prepared to throw away.

3. I will not abandon him now that he's 68 years old, forcing him to live in a bed-sit on his own. Here I detect an old habit of mine: the 'fixer', the 'protector', the 'rescuer': I "have" to look after him; I am sure I can handle the sorrow of my separateness and disconnection from Jim but I "know" that he, at 68 years plus, would find being completely alone far more difficult. I'm sure he would have been able to, had I not barged into his life all those years ago but not anymore, not after having lived together for more than 37 years.

4. The fourth factor, and from the purely practical point of view, is that I have never lived alone. I'm not afraid (at least, I don't think I am) and I do enjoy my own company. Besides, I have been alone for most of my married life. What does cause me real anxiety is that I have never had to cope with the practicalities of day-to-day living like changing a light bulb or a fuse, sorting out a leaky tap or a crashed computer.

So here I am – it's this 'either/or' again: either I stay with him or I leave him – and both options strike me as deeply unsatisfactory.

☆ ☆ ☆ ☆ ☆ ☆

Since my previous notes a couple of weeks ago something amazing has happened. Everything has changed; I have changed. Something happened that caused this "switch" in me which, as usual, I can't explain but that feels absolutely true and right deep down in my body.

I looked at Jim as if I were seeing him for the very first time and it was as if the fog had suddenly cleared. "It's time for me to be happy". I finally saw that Jim is not, in the true sense of the word, my husband and has not been for many, many years. He is – and I am now willing to recognise and accept this truth – a lodger; we share a house, we get on well and he does contribute in his own way but that is the extent of our relationship.

I have no idea what sparked the realisation. Possibly it's something I have known for a long time but would not admit to myself. What I find fascinating is that this new awareness is my sub-conscious at work. I'm convinced that my real Self is asserting itself over the fears and deceptions of my False Self.

Suddenly seeing what has been the truth for such a long time seems nothing short of miraculous to me and is incredibly freeing. The freedom comes from knowing that any expectations I may have of a lodger are completely different from those of a life partner.

My needs and expectations of Jim have been unrealistic and unreasonable, given who he is and who he has always been, and this new insight means that now I will never again be disappointed.

This change in perception opens a whole new world for me. I am now free to open myself up to life and everything and anything it may bring.

☆ ☆ ☆ ☆ ☆ ☆

It's now April, two weeks since I wrote the above and I have moved on yet again. It is true that my perception of Jim has changed; that is in no doubt but, since this change in me happened I have been noticing other things. I have begun to feel rather uncomfortable when I'm with him, because my behaviours have not changed. I had omitted to do something really fundamental: Tell Jim of my new perception of him. As usual, I'm doing it all on my own. Why? The obvious thought that springs to mind is that by telling him, I will make it real and I don't feel adequately prepared for the consequences. I have not resolved the issues that keep me "in my place". Simply thinking of him as a 'lodger' in my own mind doesn't automatically stop my expectations. There is more to it than that.

I see now that there are various mechanisms I use to maintain the status quo – both in my inner and my outer reality:

1. I use emotionally loaded terms to keep myself oppressed, for example: "I will not abandon him, now that he's old, forcing him to live in a bed-sit on his own." Not only does this thought keep me "down"; I find it absolutely abhorrent because it doesn't fit in with my self-image of a good, loving and caring person. Besides, I have had it drummed into me never to deliberately hurt another person.

2. I scare myself silly about not knowing how to handle the practicalities of day-to-day living. Even my Mum, who was 71 when widowed, learned to deal with the

everyday matters that come up when living alone.

3. Looking back I have systematically left dealing with normal everyday matters to Jim. I concentrated on earning our living and left everything else to him and now I'm afraid I wouldn't be able to handle what millions of other people do.

Of course, I haven't always been the sole breadwinner. When Jim and I were first married we both had jobs. The reason he looked after everything else then was because I tended to regard it as a man's job. My Dad took also took care of these things and it never occurred to me that Jim would not. Besides, he genuinely enjoyed it and was good at it.

4. Finally, there is the fact that I love him. And why shouldn't I? Having lived together for more than 37 years yes, there is a strong feeling of familiarity and affection even tenderness, between us. But this could be a plus point. I learned a long time ago that it doesn't matter what I do that makes a difference – it's how I do it. The same applies to ending my relationship with Jim. I have no wish to end it in anger, accusations and resentment. Behaving non-lovingly towards others is no different to behaving non-lovingly towards myself. But I have no doubt there will be much pain, on both sides.

So, what next? I need to learn to be independent so I'm starting the process by setting myself a programme to learn about running a home. I don't want to think any further just yet, but I hope that, once I'm in the process, the momentum will carry me along.

As I have already repeatedly pointed out, seeing the truth means there is nowhere left to hide. It implies a certain finality and yet, it is liberating because self-deception and denial have always kept me stuck. And only when I know what's true can I do something about it. I cannot run away from my feelings of sadness; I have to experience them so they can cleanse and heal me. I have wasted so much time and energy living a life of pretence, which not only failed to make me happy but also prevented me from doing what was needed to find genuine happiness.

Facing the truth has brought up in me feelings of anxiety and sometimes even a longing for the familiar and the fake sense of security that comes from living in fantasy-land. I can sense the danger of sliding back again into yet another month, another year, another decade of frustration, resentment and feeling misunderstood; in short, feeling unloved. Fortunately, I have come too far to turn back now.

☆ ☆ ☆ ☆ ☆ ☆

It's June now and the last two months feel like a blur. Having made the decision to leave Jim I'm overwhelmed with feelings of grief. It feels very different from the feelings of sadness I felt all these years. It just hurts so much; it's all I can do to keep going. I've told my Mum and some of my closest friends and they're all one hundred percent behind me. I'm glad about that because it means I don't have to spend a lot of time and energy defending and justifying my decision. I also made it absolutely clear to them that I'm not doing this because Jim is a villain; he's not – it's just that it's now time for truth and genuine love in my life – not from another man but Love. I've come to know the hard way that living a lie blocks love and I don't want this anymore. But that doesn't stop the grief nor, as I know somewhere deep inside, should it.

I'm not yet ready to say anything to Jim because I don't know what it all means in practice. I don't even know what it involves to apply for divorce. How long would it take? What would the financial implications be? What about the house? Where am I going to live? Can I afford a place on my own? Where is Jim going to live? Can he afford a place for himself? What's going to happen him? All I have is questions, and scary ones at that. They keep going round and round in my head and I don't know where to turn to find the answers.

☆ ☆ ☆ ☆ ☆ ☆

I was making coffee in the office kitchen the other day, when I noticed a leaflet on the wall about the company's Employee Assistance Programme. Funny, I'd never really noticed it before. I went in early one day last week and called them. They have a financial adviser and he was incredibly helpful, very kind and patient. I could barely get the words out without bursting into tears. He gave me a lot of useful advice so now I know where to make a start.

Apart from the financial and legal implications, I can't help worrying about Jim. I'm still not able to let go of this, so I've also been making enquiries about accommodation possibilities on his behalf. A friend suggested this is something Jim needs to do for himself, but I can't let it be. I need to know these things so I can be as sure as possible that he will be all right – for my own peace of mind and also, I suppose, to ease my feelings of guilt about taking his home away from him, especially now that he's old.

☆ ☆ ☆ ☆ ☆ ☆

I've been really worried about what it takes to get a divorce so this morning I again came in early to call the Employee Assistance Programme people. That was a strange experience.

The woman explained that it would take five years' separation if Jim contests it and two years with his agreement. I sat there in disbelief and numbness. Then I thought, 'God would never have brought me this far only to dump me – no way'.

"What is a quickie divorce?", I asked.

In a casual, almost dismissive tone of voice she replied "Oh, that's just in the case of unreasonable behaviour" – *JUST?!?!?*

I hung up and sat there, hardly able to breathe. There is hope.

☆ ☆ ☆ ☆ ☆ ☆

I'm worried about finding a solicitor who will not take a confrontational approach. I know exactly how I want to do this – everything 50-50. I have decided that I don't want Jim to go into rented accommodation because then his savings would run out. How would he continue paying for a place to live? I have to make sure he has enough money from the sale of the house to buy a flat outright. I have no idea if that's possible not knowing how much we would get for our house. But first, I need a solicitor.

☆ ☆ ☆ ☆ ☆ ☆

Alan gave me the name of a solicitor who specialises in divorce. From what he told me, I like the sound of her. I suppose the next step is to make an appointment to find out where I stand.

☆ ☆ ☆ ☆ ☆ ☆

This morning I phoned the solicitor to make an appointment. I can't believe my feelings of grief. I was crying whilst talking with her but she was all right about it. She told me this is perfectly normal. I thought it would be a liberating step and that I would feel really good about it, but I don't. I'm feeling incredibly sad and vulnerable. It all now looks so "real".

☆ ☆ ☆ ☆ ☆ ☆

Last Monday I went to see the solicitor. She was great. She must have had hundreds of middle-aged women come through her office in the same situation but I didn't feel patronised for a single moment. I was deeply shocked to discover just how easy it is to get a divorce although, at the same time, I'm feeling so very relieved that I don't have to wait years, as I'd first been told. She also suggested I talk to my financial adviser about how to raise as much capital as possible so both Jim and I can buy a place of our own. She thought it would be possible. That, too, felt reassuring.

Whilst all this is going on I'm spending a lot of the time crying. As I walk to the station, it is still dark and completely empty so I can cry to my heart's content without feeling inhibited about making a noise or calling attention to myself. I find the crying releases a lot of emotional pressure. Afterwards, I can breathe again. In the office, I'm functioning. I told my manager, Andrew, what I'm doing because the grief was pouring out of my body and I could no longer keep it secret. I feel really blessed with him and my other work colleagues who are being incredibly supportive in their own ways – mostly by not coming over to me expecting confidences. They just let me be which I find very helpful. Andrew keeps checking up on me to see how I'm doing. It matters enormously to me that he really cares.

To my surprise, I'm still doing a good job. It's quite amazing. It's as if there were two of me. The one who's talking to clients in a light-hearted way and the one who's watching me doing it. Sometimes, the pressure and the effort are so heavy I can barely hold myself together but my sales figures show that, somehow, I do.

☆ ☆ ☆ ☆ ☆ ☆

I've started clearing out the little guest room because I've decided that, as soon as I tell Jim that I'm leaving him, I will move in there. Interestingly, he hasn't asked why I'm suddenly putting so much effort into it, not one word.

☆ ☆ ☆ ☆ ☆ ☆

I have decided to take a radical step. I have taken off my wedding ring. I wonder if Jim will notice.

☆ ☆ ☆ ☆ ☆ ☆

A week has passed and Jim hasn't said a word. I don't know if he has noticed and chosen not to comment or if he hasn't even noticed.

☆ ☆ ☆ ☆ ☆ ☆

Yet another week has passed and I have finally decided it's time to tell Jim. It has to be on a weekend because I don't want to just tell him and then run away to work or tell him before I'm off to bed. It will definitely be next Sunday.

☆ ☆ ☆ ☆ ☆ ☆

The way I'm feeling right now, I wish it were all over and done with. It's particularly hard being around him, knowing what I've decided yet still going through the same routine.

☆ ☆ ☆ ☆ ☆ ☆

It's Monday evening and I told him yesterday. I was amazed at my firmness and determination, particularly in the face of his reaction: initial disbelief, followed by fear about what was going to happen to him.

I've threatened to leave him several times but this was completely different. In the past he would tell me how much he loved me and that we could work it out – which turned out to mean, I could do whatever I liked as long as it didn't involve him. But he also knew that I wouldn't go through with it. I think this time he knew I meant it because he didn't say anything to try and change my mind, other than to panic. I had correctly anticipated his panic reaction, which made no difference whatsoever to my determination to go through with it. But it's grim, particularly as I can't leave; I have nowhere to go, not until the house is sold.

Immediately after I told him I moved into the little guest-room. "Little" is the operative word but I'll manage.

☆ ☆ ☆ ☆ ☆ ☆

It's July now and 2½ weeks have passed since I told Jim. Watching him suffer is incredibly painful. All my old habitual ways of wanting to deal with other people's pain have surfaced, particularly wanting to fix it for them by shielding, saving, rescuing and protecting them. One particularly insidious habit stands out, where I tell myself that others need protecting because they can't handle "it". I thought I'd long left it behind. Feeling his distress as well as my own is harrowing.

There is such a deep conflict going on: on the one hand I want to "mother" him, "make it all better" and take away his pain – especially his fear. On the other, being with him in the same room feels incredibly stressful, so I keep wanting to escape. He moves from deep fear and panic, turning himself into the victim and me into the villain, to appearing perfectly all right again. I never know in what emotional state I'm going to find him when I get back from work.

However, since I have nowhere else to go, I must stay in the same house until it is sold and this may take several months. The whole process of detaching myself emotionally is turning out to be harder than even I ever imagined it would be. Anticipating something and experiencing it are clearly very different things. Besides, I do care about him and we have been together for most of my adult life.

I'm still expressing old self-damaging habits and I've realised only this morning that, despite my intention not to, I am giving out mixed messages. My words are absolutely uncompromising and straight but my actions may be confusing. I still share some meals with him, which he cooks. I seem to be detaching myself from him in stages – I just feel unable to do it all at once.

I have been putting myself under pressure to go through this process perfectly and with the highest integrity from day one, being critical when I fail to live up to my own expectations of my conduct. Another non-loving action.

One positive and helpful thing I have been doing is trying to visualise what my very own home is going to look and feel like – a place where I will truly belong. I have been taking an "it will be all right when (whatever)" approach, in this case, when I finally move into my new home. However, I do have a new, albeit temporary, home right now, the little guest-room. As Alan perceptively said, I have done nothing to create my very own space even though I expect to live there for the next two or three months. It is still just a room with a bed, a chest of drawers and a little night table.

Getting the house sorted and ready to put on the market looms like a huge obstacle. And it's difficult to get a handle on it. Things are not progressing at all. I tell myself Jim is totally resistant so nothing gets done. Admittedly understandable. After all what represents progress for me means loss to him. Yet another area where I need to take charge. I notice I haven't done anything to truly move things forward because it feels cruel to push. How is that for self-sabotage? I really can't go on like this.

☆ ☆ ☆ ☆ ☆ ☆

Once I became aware of what I've been doing or rather, not doing, about creating a special place for myself in my new bedroom, I penned a motto: "the future is now". Ever since I have been taking some small steps to make this room feel different. I put up pictures which Niki gave me, including a collage of what my new place will feel like – created by her. I see it when I first wake up in the morning. I have flowers, a little portable telly which she also gave me, a video recorder and my radio so I can put music on first thing in the morning. And I sit in silence for anything between 15 and 20 minutes. Sitting peacefully with my thoughts feels really good.

☆ ☆ ☆ ☆ ☆ ☆

In my heart of hearts I have always known it is a good (if sometimes painful) thing for Jim to feel all his feelings, especially those from which I have tried to shield him all these years (fear, uncertainty, worry, anxiety, pain). But watching him experience them without interfering is harder than I ever imagined.

Just because I am the one who initiated the separation doesn't make the experience any less painful.

☆ ☆ ☆ ☆ ☆ ☆

I am being really hard on Jim about him not doing enough to get the place ready – without noticing that he has actually been making real progress. He was angry and hurt and I did apologise to him from the bottom of my heart. I saw that I was being critical and unfair because I'm feeling anxious and impatient. Jim seems to show his feelings more now than he ever did. I wonder why that is? Perhaps he feels he's got nothing more to lose? But, of course, I'm only guessing. I spent all these years wondering what he really felt and now I'm beginning to get a few glimpses here and there. I wonder how things would have turned out if he had been able to express his feelings before we reached this point.

When I first started on this journey – separating from Jim – I intended to come from a good place, a place of love.

As the process continues, however, I'm finding it really difficult to know what that's like in practice. I thought it meant making absolutely sure I don't give out any mixed messages which means that I've been keeping our interactions as limited as I possibly can. Recently, when he became distressed again, I suggested he ask his doctor to be referred to a counsellor because I know from my own experience how important it is to be able to talk to someone who will really listen. He became very upset and shouted, "I'm talking to **you**!" but I replied "I'm the wrong person because I **am** the problem." This is so strange, now **he's** the one who wants to talk and I am the one who can't listen.

☆ ☆ ☆ ☆ ☆ ☆

I'm thinking of telling him why I've been avoiding him and, if he's willing to talk then I'm more than willing to listen. I have no idea if this will make any difference to him, whether he'll even want to respond or if he only wants to talk to get me to change my mind. But the real issue is my willingness to open up to him not *how* or even *if* he responds. I believe it will ease things. At the moment even breathing when I'm around him is difficult. I truly hope that this step will make it easier for us to be in the same space together without me feeling constantly sick with anxiety.

☆ ☆ ☆ ☆ ☆ ☆

This reflection comes about ten minutes after my previous ones. For the first time in what feels like a very long time, I'm experiencing a feeling of peace. I also identified two other ways I've unintentionally been non-loving towards myself: one was believing I would know how to be in this situation from day one. The other is that I haven't allowed myself to acknowledge how much I will actually miss him. I wrongly believed that admitting it to myself would mean that I'm doubting the soundness of my decision to leave him.

☆ ☆ ☆ ☆ ☆ ☆

I did talk with Jim yesterday as intended and concluded that my original approach, staying away from him as much as possible is, in fact, the right one. When I told him that I'm leaving him he came up with platitudes such as 'This is silly'. Fine, it's silly. I'm out of here anyway. 'You're throwing everything away'. Throwing *what* away. This is the best he can do after 37 years? I don't want to hear this.

And yet the stress I'm experiencing has only partly something to do with him. It is more about behaving in a way that has always been alien to me – tough and uncompromising.

☆ ☆ ☆ ☆ ☆ ☆

Only by constantly listening to myself and to my own needs will I survive this process without becoming ill. I will find ways to look after myself, including pleasures large and small in my routine. I made a list of the things that make me happy (I was surprised how many there were) and try to include as many as practicable every day, paying attention to which activity would be particularly good for the emotional need of the moment.

Week commencing 18 August 2003

I've been very sad again. Sometimes the sadness catches me unawares and, when I feel it coming (the pressure in my chest slowly builds up) I make sure I can be alone for a few minutes and just cry. This is what enables me to keep functioning as well as I am.

I've been re-reading my previous reflections about all the non-loving qualities I expressed in my marriage in response to Jim's distant behaviour.

Whilst it was all true, it is still only part of the story. Those were not the only qualities I displayed – I also brought a lot of love, certainly unlimited good intentions and a lot of effort. And Jim, too, was not only the distant, withholding and resistant person I have painted him to be. He was also deeply patient and caring, not only when I was ill or in physical pain but also with Papi, especially when he noticed the lump. I will never forget it.

He was also very nourishing in his own way; he loved cooking meals he thought I would enjoy. Occasionally, he'd play my favourite music when I came home from work. I genuinely enjoyed those gestures and I always told him so fully knowing his deepest need is to be appreciated. I didn't always need words from him. There were times when I'd feel content and glad to be with him.

I'm not sure why I'm weeping as I'm writing this. No, that's not true. I do know. We both loved each other very much (and still do). How sad that neither of us loved the other in the way we needed to be loved.

In the end, being loved only in the way he was willing and/or able was not enough and hence such deep sadness. I wonder if he felt the same about my way of loving him. I used to ask him but he would assure me everything was fine although I never did quite believe him. Even now I don't know – and I don't suppose I ever will.

☆ ☆ ☆ ☆ ☆ ☆

It's been a few days since I recorded my last reflections and I'm thinking, "What am I doing, idealising a false way of loving? A way of loving that caused me to pretend I was content when I wasn't? Happy when I wasn't? Not hurt when I was? That I didn't mind whatever it was when I did? Always wishing it were different, that *he* were different and hoping he would change? Is that what I'm sad about?

But those were my pretences, not his. As I dig deeper I recognise that I learned to pretend when I was a child – expressing anger, disappointment or frustration were strongly discouraged, as was expressing what I was truly feeling, especially if my feelings were negative. Nobody forced me to pretend; I was terrified that expressing my truth would lead to rejection. As it turned out, the exact opposite was true. It was pretending and deceiving myself – and, therefore, deceiving Jim – that landed me in this situation. I also had expectations of him, of how he should be, in the same way my parents had expectations of me. But knowing this doesn't change the fact that I feel angry and hurt.

I now know that ours was not love in the true sense. There is only one way I want to be and that is truthful. My friend Gill, whom I've known for years, asked me recently if I was all right. I haven't told her yet that I'm separating from Jim; I didn't feel ready to tell her. I also didn't want to pretend I was alright when I wasn't. I replied

"Actually, no, I'm not"

"Is it work?", she asked

"No", I said, "but I don't really want to talk about it right now."

That simple expression of what was true for me was just right. If I'd said "Yes, I'm fine," as I used to in similar circumstances, then I would have continued to feel burdened because pretence is a heavy burden. As it was, there was no pressure. I'd been truthful yet chosen not disclose something before I was ready to do so. I'm learning that being truthful doesn't necessarily mean revealing all.

☆ ☆ ☆ ☆ ☆ ☆

A lot of work needs to be done on the house to make it saleable and it will be impossible to get on with it while Jim is around. Earlier in the year, before I'd even thought of leaving, we booked a holiday. It is obvious now that we won't be going away together but I encouraged him to consider going on his own. Eventually, he agreed.

I also booked some time off to coincide with him being away. I have planned major projects. For a start, removing the wallpaper in the living room, painting the walls and getting rid of an enormous bush in front of the living room window which makes it look and feel dark and oppressive.

☆ ☆ ☆ ☆ ☆ ☆

I've really been looking forward to the holiday but, as the time approaches I'm beginning to feel anxious about the amount of work involved. I'm looking around me and have no idea where and how to start. I'm afraid I'll waste my precious time off. Speaking to Niki about my worries, she understood immediately. She explained it was because I had never done any painting and decorating before, and so I had no frame of reference, nothing to tell me how straight-forward it really was. Two things came to mind as she was talking – first, I'd been trying really hard to suppress my fear. Then, as she went on talking, I felt soothed. It's as if I can breathe again.

She suggested I spend tomorrow afternoon (Saturday) at her place. That will be really great.

Week commencing 25 August 2003

This has been a strange week so far. I've been feeling peaceful and happy. I think it's the anticipation of Jim being away. I will finally be able to breathe! Whenever I'm around him I seem to be holding my breath. So just the idea of him not being around feels like such relief! I even managed to cope with some setbacks without getting upset or frustrated. Even better, when a problem comes up, instead of panicking I just deal with it.

Take, for example, all the things that need to be thrown away. I'd arranged to hire a skip. Then, just as I was about to leave work on Monday I got a call telling me that the skip had been refused a licence. I went numb. I thought "This can't be. What am I going to do now?". Fortunately, I told Simon, a colleague, what had just happened and he advised me to contact another company who come and collect rubbish.

I got home just after 6:00 having missed my train but I thought I'd try to sort this out straight away. Quite by chance (chance?) I found out that the same company who were to organise the skip also do waste management. I managed to find the manager, rearrange things and now they will be coming on Thursday next week which is the first day of my holiday. This will mean advance planning rather than having a whole week to "amble" through the process. Perhaps this is a "cleaner" approach. I'm just relieved I've sorted this out.

☆ ☆ ☆ ☆ ☆ ☆

Week commencing 1 September 2003

This morning it dawned on me that there are only four days left before Jim goes on holiday and I was overcome by panic. So much to do, I'm completely paralysed with anxiety. As soon as I got to work I phoned Jim and shouted that if he didn't get rid of all the stuff then I would. He must know by now that I wasn't bluffing. I went on and on at him. He told me calmly that there was plenty of time to sort it all out. I didn't feel particularly reassured. Afterwards I called my Mum still sobbing over the phone until eventually I calmed down.

☆ ☆ ☆ ☆ ☆ ☆

I really don't know what's going on with me today. I'm feeling as weepie as I did in the early weeks. At lunchtime I went to St. Martin's Church on Piccadilly, just around the corner from work and carried on crying, but it hasn't made any difference. I don't know what this is all about, although it feels more like sadness than fear. I wonder if it's got anything to do with the fact that today is the two months' "anniversary" of the day I told Jim I was going to leave him. Oh sod it!

☆ ☆ ☆ ☆ ☆ ☆

I've been watching some "house doctor" programmes that Niki recorded for me, so that I could understand what needs doing to make it more appealing to potential buyers. I have to say, I now understand what she's been talking about but it does seem overwhelming without a team of specialists at my beck and call. I'm feeling anxious that I won't use my time productively because I know nothing about painting and decorating. I don't feel at all prepared but, one way or another I will have to deal with it; I don't have any choice.

☆ ☆ ☆ ☆ ☆ ☆

In the course of clearing up, I found eight journals that I kept from February 1981 to December 1998. Today I decided to read them, starting with my very first one.

Why was I so shaken to read experiences recorded over 23 years ago that are as true today as they were then? Perhaps because I had started to wonder if things were really as empty and lonely as I remembered them, if I really did tell him how I felt, if I really did try hard enough. My unlimited capacity for self-deception was truly shocking : "I know he loves me and I love him so much" written time and again, in between recordings of the many ways I've felt estranged, rejected, even humiliated by his lack of interest, as if I were intruding into his life and beating at the brick walls surrounding him, begging him to let me in.

How on earth did I ever believe myself to be loved?!?!

☆ ☆ ☆ ☆ ☆ ☆

Something amazing has happened! My anxiety had reached fever pitch and I was crying into the phone to my friend Toria.

"How will I ever be able to sort the house!", I wailed.

"Do you need another pair of hands?", she asked. How about that!

I sniffled for another few seconds before I said, "Yes, please!"

My Goodness! I can hardly believe that I won't have to do this on my own.

☆ ☆ ☆ ☆ ☆ ☆

It's now 9:00 PM and Jim has left on his holidays. I just cannot believe what I've done. I told him to take the house keys with him because I would be at work when he arrived back. I told him! It was the last thing I said to him! Anyway, only minutes after he left I saw he'd left the keys behind. And, what I cannot believe is that I have just run after him to make sure he has the bloody keys! I actually ran after him!

The whole day was most unusual. I heard Jim start to get the stuff ready for collection at 4:00 a.m. and he's continued working pretty much for the next 12 hours. I worked hard alongside him and it gave the whole thing this strange sense of teamwork. And yet we have never worked as a team, we never had a common life goal. I feel sad that we had to reach this stage before working as a team. I wonder what he's feeling. I suppose I could interpret his hard work as being driven by a sense of emergency. Alternatively, since I'm staying behind, perhaps he wanted to make sure I didn't have to deal with this lot by myself. I wish I knew.

As the time for him to leave was drawing nearer I felt odd. I'm not sure how to describe 'odd' – I suppose a little sad and uncertain about what's to come, meaning what it will "look" and feel like.

The irritation with myself has now drained away leaving me exhausted, so I had better go to bed. I imagine tomorrow is the beginning of my new life.

Week commencing 8 September 2003

8 September *(Day 1 on my own)*

Yesterday I got up much earlier than planned. I felt – free, enjoying having the place to myself even though it looks like a bomb site. The plan was for Niki, my "house doctor" friend, to come over and take a professional and objective view of the house. In the end we spent just over nine hours together.

It was a really strange day. Every once in a while I continued to beat myself up for running after Jim with the house keys. I really have to stop this. This self-punishment I thought I'd left behind is doing me no good at all. It's very non-loving.

The other thing I found very difficult was having Niki, in her role of "house doctor", cast a completely detached eye over every nook and cranny and every item of furniture and accessories. Her whole focus was how to make this property really appealing to potential buyers. To me, it was a ruthless diagnosis. She pointed to pieces of furniture that absolutely must go to create a greater sense of light and space and, as she was talking, I became aware of a deep sense of resistance and vulnerability.

On reflection, this feels very much like a previous experience I had. I had spent weeks and weeks processing grief and sadness following my decision to separate from Jim and doing a lot of research about what this would mean in practice, both for him and for me. When I finally made the phone call to the solicitor to make an appointment I felt emotionally raw. I later recognised that was the call that made it all become real and tangible whereas before I had been merely processing it all in my head.

I'm also experiencing most unhelpful feelings of somehow being disloyal to Jim. I've been telling him for weeks to get rid of certain pieces of furniture because they will just not fit into his new space. Yet now I feel guilty for getting rid of them. His strategy is to keep as much as possible and then only get rid of whatever he can't fit in into his new home. I can't wait to sell the house and start my new life so why am I feeling so resistant? I think it's yet another step closer to our final separation; to the end of my life as I've known it. I will do whatever it takes to get this house ready.

After her diagnosis, Niki listed the various items I need to get me started and, as I listened to her reeling off the list I actually felt a sense of anticipation and excitement. We then went to our local B&Q and filled up the trolley. It was great.

And finally, the highlight of the day was a visit to John Lewis for a visual treat of what pictures and accessories might make the house more appealing. I fell in love with a painting of a blue sky with wispy clouds over a calm sea. Just looking at it makes me feel peaceful. Not only will it come with me to my new home but I've already hung it up in my little room, my new home, for the time being.

In two days' time I start my annual leave and the plan is to get the place ready for painting and decorating. I'm not exactly sure what that involves but I will find out soon enough.

9 September *(Day 2 on my own)*

I went to work today. Yesterday was a day of mixed emotions – from the exhilarated and excited to the vulnerable and anxious. But today is today and, at work at least, I had a particularly good day though I felt sick with anxiety. The good news is that the waste management people are coming tomorrow as is Toria, my "extra pair of hands" so, really, I don't know why I should feel anxious – but I do.

10 September *(Day 3 on my own)*

I've had the most incredible day, one of those days that I experience only very occasionally – as if Somebody switches the light on and I am no longer in darkness.

It started with all the rubbish being collected, so the front of the house looks clear again. That brought an immediate sense of relief.

Then came "the big one": I actually arranged for a charity to collect the three items of furniture that Niki and I had identified for disposal. I had been deeply worried about the possibility of not being able to get rid of them before Jim came back and then the struggle and resistance would be on again and I simply couldn't bear the thought. Now it will all be sorted by next week. The feeling of relief and freedom is enormous even though I know Jim will be very upset.

Next, my friend Toria arrived. She and I managed to do some tasks which I had regarded as absolutely impossible. She's an amazing person. It was only later that I found out she had never done a project this size before. But she has a wonderful "have a go – how hard can it be?" attitude that is absolutely infectious. Between us, we heaved and carried, pulled and pushed the most awkward and challenging tasks into submission.

The next milestone was that I cooked lunch for both of us – a very, very simple lunch. It was the symbolism rather than the actual meal because, in fact, I haven't had to cook anything for about twenty years. That was always Jim's responsibility.

We also hired a wallpaper stripper. Niki was a little worried when I told her, but it's too late now to draw back – so, fingers crossed.

I'm now aching all over while Toria just skipped off. But the sense of wonder, well-being, triumph and excitement is all I care about right now. Next, a hot, leisurely bath.

11 September *(Day 4 on my own)*

Today was quite different from yesterday – stripping the wallpaper was slow, hard work – the wallpaper was very old so that might explain it. All in all, it was both satisfying and frustrating.

On a different note, I prepared a fantastic couscous dish (under Toria's gentle guidance). What surprised me is that I don't feel at all awkward in the kitchen. I found I did remember bits and pieces about how to handle things. Such a contrast to all those years ago when someone commented that I cooked like a laboratory technician, measuring everything very precisely. This time I experimented, guessed roughly how much of this or that should go into the dish and it felt more fun and liberating. This is so unlike me!

The other thing I noticed is that my body isn't aching at all – not even my back. This is nothing short of a miracle. Again, this is so unlike me!

12 September *(Day 5 on my own)*

We're still working on the living/dining room and I've started dreading not being able to finish it before Jim comes back from his holidays. After a very slow-moving morning still stripping the wallpaper in the living room Toria suggested that we needed a different tool so I went over to Sandra, a neighbour. As she was looking through the toolbox she asked how I was and, quite unexpectedly, I burst into tears and told her what was going on. She was very sympathetic, found the tool and came over to have a look at what we were up to. Then she told me her husband was a painter/decorator – and I never knew! Jim and I have lived here for twenty-two years and I never knew! Toria and I went back to work and, with the new tool things progressed much faster.

In the evening Reg, our newly discovered painter neighbour, came to have a look at our efforts, shaking his head most of the time, although he did say that we'd done extremely well to get as far as we had. He said he would ask a couple of his mates if they're willing to lend a hand – for a price, of course, and he himself will come and help next weekend – before I start work again. This was not the moment to think about saving the pennies. Time is of the essence. I've decided to accept the offers of professional help so that the work can be finished after my leave is over.

☆ ☆ ☆ ☆ ☆ ☆

I'm getting mixed messages from estate agents. Some tell me the house is virtually unsaleable unless I replace the kitchen and the bathroom. Others tell me not to bother because the new owners will want to choose their own style. All I know is that I need to be as sure as I possibly can be that we can ask the highest price this kind of property can command. After splitting the proceeds 50-50, both Jim and I will need to find a decent place to live. I just don't know what to do. But then I think – it will be all right. I know I'm being looked after and all has gone smoothly so far. Even the setbacks, with the benefit of hindsight, have turned out to be beneficial.

I have also had a foretaste of what it will be like living on my own and faced with domestic problems. I ask someone for help – and it's there.

The most important thing about this experience so far has been my constant refrain "This is so unlike me!": I'm doing physical and strenuous work I've never done before and not only am I doing it competently, but also I am feeling very good physically. I've started cooking simple meals and am enjoying the experience – they taste very good indeed. I'm thinking in new and creative ways to resolve problems and situations I've never been in before – and they work. Soon this refrain "This is so unlike me!" will have to become – "This is who I am now".

From tomorrow I'll be working completely on my own for the next four days. True to my old habits, I am worried.

12 September *(Day 6 on my own)*

Today was the strangest and most amazing day in my whole life. It started with my doing really good work, emptying the three cabinets to be collected tomorrow by the charity, and finding a home for everything that I felt was OK to keep. I was about to start with the wallpaper stripping when Sandra dropped by to see how I was doing and tell me that "she'd rallied the troops". What she then said was nothing short of a miracle.

She and her husband had arranged for three of their decorator mates to come over tomorrow evening and work a couple of hours on the living room, sort out the worst in the kitchen, and carry on with everything until the work was done. An electrician would also come round and have a look at some weak spots. And all at half price because it's between friends.

Sandra lent me tools for clearing up the garden rubbish and cutting back overgrown bushes. She made some excellent suggestions about creating more space in the kitchen.

My response? I burst into tears and hugged her.

Sandi works part-time: Mondays and Fridays are her days off. Tomorrow she'll come to collect me and we'll get the paint, return the wallpaper stripper, buy provisions for the men and whatever else is needed.

After she left I felt numb. I couldn't take it all in so I just carried on working and focusing all my energies on the job. It was only later when I called Niki to tell her all about it that I burst into tears.

I'm trying to figure out what I'm feeling and the only word that springs to mind is 'overwhelmed'.

13 September *(Day 7 on my own)*

I still felt overwhelmed and vulnerable this morning when the charity collected the two living room dressers; it doesn't matter to me that the narrow one in my bedroom has gone as well but the other two – that's different. After the men left I thought "Oh, my God! What have I done?!" I know it was necessary but I still feel vulnerable. It was such a major thing to do. I'm also feeling apprehensive about Jim's reaction. That, too, is confusing. Why should it matter? Why can't I stop caring? Oh, damn!

And that's not the only thing I feel confused about. I expected to feel exhilarated and excited about all the help I'm getting, instead of which I feel vulnerable, overwhelmed and sometimes weepie. At least the tiredness is not surprising. I'm discovering just how wonderful people are. I don't think I ever really knew. Well, it's not that I didn't know, rather I never really thought much about it. I had never asked for help before and now, when I do, they're there for me. Isn't that something!

Despite all this inner and outer turbulence I feel satisfied with progress and there are moments when I catch myself enjoying it all. I keep surprising myself – the way I'm applying my skills to such a completely unfamiliar and daunting situation. There are moments when it appears quite overwhelming – and then I find myself dealing with it, step by step and moving forwards.

I'm so pleased to have found yet more ways of creating space, this time in the living room. I found stuff of my own I don't mind getting rid of. I still don't feel I've done enough but I'm so tired I've just stopped.

14 September *(Day 8 on my own)*
I'm absolutely exhausted; my body aches all over and yet I feel deeply satisfied.
I started my morning by going shopping. The sun was shining and I hadn't been out much lately.

I cannot get over how rewarding scrubbing and cleaning can be. I was actually having a good time. I wouldn't want to be anywhere else other than where I am right now.

All these years I felt the house looked and felt unloved. I never realised that it was a symbol for me who was unloved. That's why regardless of what I did to make a difference nothing ever worked. So I eventually stopped even trying. But now it's different. I'm pouring all my love into this work and it shows. The love is for the new life I'm creating for myself and every step I take reflects that.

15 September *(Day 9 on my own)*
This morning I'm feeling anxious: I only have four "working" days left of my holidays – I'm taking Saturday off for a special treat. I called Niki to discuss how to use the remaining time most productively. She thought I need to accept that the living/dining room will not be completely finished before Jim comes back. which, I could see she was right, but I was upset. With the biggest tasks being done by the professionals: painting ceilings, walls, doors and so on, she reassured me, everything else would be much easier although it won't all be finished overnight.

We then talked about my anxiety about Jim's reaction. I had lost sight of the reason behind the whole project. I'm doing this so that we can get a better price for the house. All this work is for both of us and so, if he's upset and angry, then he will just have to get over it. I can't believe I have been so non-loving towards myself and, with the anxiety dissipated, I am feeling much clearer. Afterwards I walked in the warm sunshine to B&Q and bought a lamp for the upstairs hallway. It has three spotlights so it will be really light and bright.

In the afternoon I did yet another thing I have never done before: I pruned two very overgrown trees, which were crowding out the garden. I'm not sure how good a job I've made of it but it's a start. I'm really whacked. It's only 4:00 o'clock but I'm calling it a day.

16 September *(Day 10 on my own)*
Today the weather is hot and radiantly sunny so I decided to take the day off. What an excellent decision. I had a wonderfully relaxing and enjoyable time without the slightest feeling of guilt. Brilliant!

17 September *(Day 11 on my own)*
I am absolutely whacked – have I said this before? It's been an amazing day – Sandi and I put the living room together again and it looks *beautiful!* We were on our hands and knees cleaning and polishing and sweeping and putting the furniture back again – in a different way from before and, of course, there's much less of it. The room looks

bright and light and big! So different from its previous dark, dingy and oppressive feel.

Then, after lunch, just when I thought my body was about to give out, Sandi suggested – "how about tackling the big bush in front of the living room?" Well, I never got my second wind back so fast. We wrestled determinedly with this mini-jungle that had kept the room in gloomy darkness for so many years and removed at least half of it. I felt rather sad because I knew we were at the same time removing Jim's defences and somehow exposing him to the light. He will be distressed about that.

It's gone 7:00 o'clock and I'm yearning for a bath and then something to eat.

Tomorrow I'm going to a workshop aptly called "The Seven Keys to an Effective Life" and I'm really looking forward to it.

18 September *(Day 12 on my own)*
I couldn't believe my eyes when I got up this morning and opened the curtains in the living room. Sandi and her team have taken down the whole bush – the whole lot! All of it! As if it had never been there. And I was so deeply asleep that I heard nothing. I stood there looking at the huge empty space saying "Oh, my Goodness!" over and over again. I feel absolutely overwhelmed at being at the receiving end of so much loving care. I can't think of another way of describing this, and indeed everything else that has happened since the beginning of my break, other than as a true miracle. The way it all came together from apparently nowhere, in my time of deepest need.

19 September *(Day 13 on my own)*
Today is the last day of my break. I've been spending it mostly catching up. It's been a quiet day, a "catching my breath" sort of day.

Tomorrow I'm back at work. I'm not sure I'm ready for it but I know I will be once I'm there.

This is going to be an interesting and, I'm sure, challenging week. I've been thinking a lot about Jim's return from his holiday and how he will react to the changes I have made. I was about to note that, if I could have done this without causing him pain, I would have. However, just as I was about to record this thought I realised that that's my old habit of colluding with him and shielding him from reality. On further reflection I can see that what he will find on his return will make the fact of our separation all the more real to him.

22 September 2003 *(Day 14 on my own)*
Jim is due back this evening. I decided to get back a little later from work to give him time on his own to take it all in. I'm feeling uncomfortable at the thought of having him there again and not a little anxious about falling back into some of my old habits and letting myself down. I suppose I'm really wondering if I can trust myself – but then I know I can, even if I occasionally slip up.

I know he will feel devastated at the loss of the bush behind which he has been hiding all these years. The living room at the moment looks bare and not particularly welcoming. I'm *not* looking forward to his return and facing his distress but I think that, if he ever had any doubts about the fact that this separation *will* happen then this should dispel them all. Still, I'm not looking forward to it.

Yesterday I found myself feeling angry at him again and shouting at him in my head. Of course, it's not really about him; only about me. To have experienced so much pain of rejection in all areas that mattered deeply and to have done absolutely nothing about it – that's good enough reason to feel angry with myself. I'm also feeling weepie but I've decided to stop trying to analyse and understand my feelings. It is just plain exhausting.

I've been having a bet with myself that he's been fantasising about how, once I find out just how difficult it is to do all the things he's been doing for me all these years I will "come to my senses" and change my mind.

☆ ☆ ☆ ☆ ☆ ☆

Today is the day after the night before. Despite all evidence to the contrary over at least 30 years, I still harbour misguided fantasies about how Jim will react in any given situation. I was convinced, for instance, that he would be distressed by the dramatic changes in the living room and the disappearance of the bush. I was also worried about the smell of paint because of his weak chest.

Jim reacted in a totally contained way, however, showing only mild, positive reaction to everything he found. Mild reactions to anything have always been his 'speciality' which is why I never knew what he really felt about anything. Well, it's obvious that I'm not about to start now. He never even mentioned the disappearance of the bush, the one thing I thought would distress him most. His only comment was that although the living room looked "nice" I had gone "overboard a bit".

I had kept all the windows open to try and get rid of as much of the paint smell as possible but, by the time I got back, he had closed them all and never mentioned it.

I was right about him thinking I would "see sense" and change my mind, once I realised just how difficult it would be to manage on my own. The clue was when he said "why do you want to throw it all away!" and I felt the familiar weight settle on my shoulders. My first thought was, "throw what away!" but I didn't say anything. Then I remembered how light and free I felt when he first left on his holiday and I resolved not to allow myself to get sucked in. What's been really great is, my decision made, my emotional state changed and I recovered my feelings of freedom and lightness and, yes, happiness.

Week commencing 29 September 2003

Yesterday evening, a week after Jim came back from his holidays, I finally managed to get him to read the deed of separation which we both signed and had witnessed. This morning I posted the documents to the solicitor.

As soon as I put the papers in the post I was overcome with the deepest feeling of grief which should not have taken me so by surprise. Just like the time I first called the solicitor to make the appointment, the signing of the papers brings our legal and final separation that much closer and makes the whole thing even more real. I spent my lunchtime at St. Martin's Church, crying.

I know there are those who would say that this is progress and, therefore, cause for celebration and I suppose it is – but not right now. All I want to do is cry. This is yet one more step towards our final separation and I feel so sad.

Week commencing 13 October 2003

Since I first told Jim I was leaving him, we have found a way to co-exist which works well. The discomfort I used to experience when I was anywhere near him has also disappeared. I now feel relaxed. It took me a while to get there but I'm there now.

I remember thinking at some point that I'm learning a new way of loving and I now can see what this new way actually is.

I have reached a point where my relationship with Jim is now truthful and genuine without the pretence and expectations. There can also be no disappointments or wishing that he were different. I no longer try to get him to love me, nor are there any resentments when he does or doesn't do or say – whatever.

I am now listening to my own needs and wants and enjoying my new way of being. My life feels very different, like an exciting adventure even though the actual activities seem outwardly ordinary. And I notice that Jim seems to be doing the same which is why we are as relaxed and comfortable with ourselves and, therefore, with each other as it's possible to be in the circumstances. I can see that this is a different way of expressing love, maybe not as conventionally understood but it is love nonetheless. This is the closest I have come to loving him – or anyone else, for that matter – unconditionally.

Week commencing 20 October 2003

Today the deeds of separation arrived, duly processed. We're now legally separated. I don't feel any differently about this because physically nothing has yet changed – but it's now done.

☆ ☆ ☆ ☆ ☆ ☆

I've been wondering why I'm feeling as if nothing has changed and I have finally worked it out: It's because I haven't yet taken one critical step. It was Alan who first brought this up.

We have yet to separate our finances. I have avoided confronting the fact that I have to learn to live within my own means, that is, without Jim's pension. Since he turned 65 his State and private pensions have significantly boosted our disposable income. So, on the surface, the reason for my resistance seemed obvious.

The real reason, however – which I find distressing – is that I have always been in total control of our finances. There were undoubtedly some poor choices, but those were made jointly with Jim. Even in the darkest moments, though, I have managed – by hook or by crook – to get us through. Jim was never there when I needed his support and I only had myself to rely on for our survival. I can also say that I did a good job.

Once the house is sold and we each have only ourselves to look after it will be different. What makes separating our finances so scary is that I will have to share this control and work together with him on the house project, doing whatever needs doing and spending whatever needs spending – to ensure that we come as close as possible to getting our asking price. Based on past experience, I don't trust him to cooperate. Getting him to do anything has always been such hard work and now I'm afraid his usual behaviour will be an obstacle to our final goal. All I can think of is that he might stand in the way of my creating the best life I can for *myself*.

I reassure myself that this is a purely emotional reaction, not based on reality as it is today. Ever since he signed the deed of separation he has become cooperative and positive about making this happen. The difference between before and now is that now he's doing it for himself. And that's a good thing. Interestingly, I don't feel at all hurt that he wouldn't do it for me. I'm just glad we are able to work on this together.

So, as always, it's not about him; it's about me – my own fears and resentments as well as my belief that only *I* can make this happen and that Jim could use his passive resistance to sabotage me. Perhaps it's time to do a reality check.

Week commencing 27 October 2003

I've been thinking long and hard about changing my name; not just in the conventional sense of shedding my married name now that I'm separated. No. Changing my name feels deeply fundamental – it symbolises who I am not just to the outside world but, more importantly, to myself.

I've spoken to people who have changed their name – some did it privately, that is, it wasn't something they advertised but something that gave them a different perspective of themselves – the chosen name became, to them, a focus of qualities they wished to develop and express; a new beginning.

When I first started working with Alan the name Sue Plumtree came to represent everything I no longer wanted to be – someone I didn't really trust, who was deceitful, colluding, full of fear and self-doubt. But, over the years, this person grew into a woman who has let go of many of the lies and deceptions that marred her life. She has overcome her fears, stopped colluding, is learning to express her own truth by making herself emotionally vulnerable and, most importantly, learned, for the most part, to trust herself and God. In short, she shed her Mask or, at least, most of it.

This is a person I have grown to like – and the name, Sue Plumtree, reflects what she has become, what I have become and it is an ongoing process. This is not just my married name although the marriage brought the name into my life. This is a name that I have made into my own and so, after long reflection I've decided to keep it.

November 2003

Getting the house on the market has become fraught with setbacks, making me sometimes feel scared and vulnerable. This weekend I have had to confront the fact that we're going to get a lot less than I had hoped. I fear that I will lose what I long for the most: a home of my own, a home where I truly belong. In talking this fear through with Niki I realised that finding the place that is absolutely right for me is not necessarily linked to how much money I will have available. I just forgot for a while the one thing I know from past experience: that the right thing will come into my life in its own good time.

☆ ☆ ☆ ☆ ☆ ☆

Since Jim's return from his holiday I notice that he has made the house "his" again. When he went away and I started doing all the work the house actually responded; it started to feel light and bright and airy. It was wonderful!

But now, after only four weeks, it has gone back to feeling dark and oppressive and there's little I can do to make a difference because I'm out at work all day. I admit it has been getting me down. But I will not forget what an eye-opener these last few weeks working on the house have been. I now know that I am capable of creating a wonderful environment for myself; an environment which is truly mine and which supports the life I want to lead, and that has nothing to do with money.

Most of the time I'm feeling happy and peaceful and having a really good time. As from next week our new financial arrangements, that is, the separate bank accounts, become operative. It will be interesting to see how that works.

☆ ☆ ☆ ☆ ☆ ☆

I can't believe how wonderfully at peace and content I'm feeling. I'm intrigued at how my feelings towards Jim have changed.

I recall how different things were almost a year ago: then I was trying to accept my situation within this so-called relationship and coming to terms with the idea that he was not my husband and partner, certainly not emotionally, practically or in any of the important ways that make a relationship genuinely true and close. And I remember deciding that the nearest I could describe him was as a lodger and how relieved I felt when I finally recognised the truth of our relationship. The problem then was that my brain and my heart were at odds with each other. Unable to let go of feelings of disappointment or resentment when my expectations were not met, I was still wishing things were different between us.

Now I rarely feel anger. My expectations have completely dissipated and I finally do regard him as a lodger, really and truly.

I do have his best interests at heart and my original intention of making sure that he has a decent home of his own is still firmly in place. Sure, I occasionally feel frustrated and irritated by him, but that's normal in any kind of on-going interaction.

Looking back at how I used to feel about him, I wonder where it all went. In its place there is now happiness and peace, enjoyment of life and a sense of lightness and freedom which is absolutely wonderful. I feel incredibly blessed and grateful.

☆ ☆ ☆ ☆ ☆ ☆

This has been a difficult week emotionally speaking. I'm not really clear what has been going on.

The confusion only started to clear through a deeply welcome and totally unexpected visit from a friend. Emma had moved to Scotland at the beginning of the year and we lost touch with each other. There was a lot to catch up on and as I was telling her I felt that familiar pressure in my chest. I knew it was grief and sadness which I hadn't felt for some weeks. Even as I'm recording this I'm feeling increasingly weepie. All the thrashing about this week tells me that it's not all over. I wanted to believe that "it's all done and dusted" – that all this messy grieving has finally ended so I can get on with my life. Who am I kidding?

In fact, I don't have much experience of major loss except when Papi died and that was a tender experience where I held him in my arms. The loss of my marriage, however, feels completely different. There is (I nearly said "was") still much anger, pain, resentment and sadness and, no matter how long the periods during which I experience peace, joy and a sense of fun, adventure and excitement, the sadness re-surfaces when I least expect it. I still, occasionally, have arguments with Jim in my head; I find myself telling him how I feel, I accuse him of being/not being, saying/not saying, doing/not doing all sorts of things. Then I catch myself and make myself stop it – but perhaps I should let it run its course.

I commented a little earlier that all this grieving stops me getting on with my life but the reality is that I *am* getting on with my life *and* I'm also grieving as and when the feelings come up in me.

This is certainly not a tidy process so I might as well just accept it.

☆ ☆ ☆ ☆ ☆ ☆

The estate agent has just left. Jim and I have been working incredibly hard together to get the house ready to market. I have decided I don't want to wait any longer because it's getting closer and closer to Christmas – and I'm really worried that this is not a good time to sell property.

Once the 'for sale' sign goes up I will buy a bottle of champagne for Sandi and Reg to thank them for all they've done for me, particularly Sandi.

I will never forget her words when Toria and I were trying to do all the painting and I suddenly knew we would not be able to make it happen: "I will mobilise the troops", she said – and she did just that.

I really thought I'd be in a celebrating mood now that the 'for sale' sign is up except that it's quite the opposite. I'm really feeling vulnerable and scared. I suddenly thought, I'm letting go of a roof over my head and have nothing yet to replace it. Not only that – it's another step toward leaving this life, 37 years with my life partner – whatever the quality of that relationship, it has still been 37 years. No wonder I'm feeling vulnerable.

Of course, I know that my anxieties are based on fantasies but this is undeniably yet another step towards letting go of this relationship. That makes me genuinely sad.

☆ ☆ ☆ ☆ ☆ ☆

I've just come back from a very special treat. I took a day off work and spent it helping Niki celebrate her birthday. We booked ourselves into a posh hotel on a special weekend offer, so we could enjoy their amazing facilities without worrying about having to trek all the way back in the evening. The break away from my responsibilities – however short – was terrific. By the time Niki and I parted company I was practically purring with relaxed contentment.

So what? Why do I feel it necessary to even mention this? It's because of the tortuous and non-loving process I put myself through before I finally decided to do it. My usual sabotaging behaviours kicked in about what I should and shouldn't do, for example, "I should really be available in case someone wants to see the house" (even though it's the agent who's showing the property to potential buyers), "one night away doesn't really make any difference so what's the point?", "this isn't really a good time to spend money on myself." What finally tipped the balance was a recognition that I did need time to look after myself, and that it doesn't benefit anyone, least of all me, if I run myself into the ground without a break. This way of thinking is not exactly second nature to me but I've noticed that, even if I do prevaricate, I now tend to end up in the right place.

☆ ☆ ☆ ☆ ☆ ☆

Interesting: ever since Jim and I split our bank accounts we're learning to actively share and negotiate. I find that really enjoyable.

☆ ☆ ☆ ☆ ☆ ☆

In the past week, despite all the stress of having people walk around our "home" to see if it's worthy of them or not, I still feel incredibly joyful and literally overwhelmed with gratitude. This is not a consistent feeling but it's frequent and, when it comes, solid. I can't explain it nor do I wish to. What I find amazing is the absolute certainty that everything will turn out all right – in the face of no evidence at all.

☆ ☆ ☆ ☆ ☆ ☆

After only four days on the market an offer has been made, negotiated to my satisfaction and accepted.

Why is it that after every new landmark towards my ultimate goal I feel so scared?!?! One minute I know, without a shadow of a doubt, that everything will be alright and the next I feel so scared. It's not just that I haven't got a new home, which is merely a question of time; I know that. All kinds of feelings have come up in me. Jim hasn't even started looking for a place yet and the old habit of trying to take him over is trying to slip back. I remembered my promise to make sure that he would be all right. Then I realised I have already kept my promise – to do everything I could to ensure we get the best possible price for the property so each of us can afford a decent place of our own.

For a moment I believed that "ensuring he'll be all right" actually meant finding him a place (rescuing and fixing it for him) but I'm facing the fact that this is his responsibility. The money is there (or will be soon). Now it's up to him. Yet this knowledge doesn't make my discomfort go away. I have always "looked after him" though it has not always been in his best interests. What I regarded as a loving thing to do was, I now see, actually non-loving because my way of loving often disempowered him. I also recognise another reason for my discomfort: to empower him means I have to let go and this is what I find hard to do – but I must.

Even more importantly, such deep sadness has come up in me again. I can't imagine what it will be like not having him around anymore. Knowing that he's away for a fortnight's holiday is one thing, but not seeing him ever again is something else entirely. I finally allowed myself to accept that I will miss him. I didn't dare let myself even think about that before because I was afraid that might mean I made a mistake. I'm still in this "black or white" way of thinking. It's right for me to leave Jim and yet miss him at the same time. The two are not mutually exclusive.

☆ ☆ ☆ ☆ ☆ ☆

Today I had a phone call from our estate agent wanting to know how my search for a new home was coming along. It was only when I hung up that I realised what the call was all about – the buyers have no property to sell and want to move in as soon as possible.

To say that I'm feeling scared and vulnerable is to put it mildly. My imagination is running riot and all my worst fantasies feel very real. At this time of year there are few properties on the market and I know all too well the destructive decisions and choices I have made in the past while in the grip of fear. I really must get a hold on myself. This is not a pattern I want to repeat but I do feel scared.

☆ ☆ ☆ ☆ ☆ ☆

Was it only yesterday I felt so scared? Today, my fear has completely dissipated. I suddenly thought "sod it – if they withdraw from the sale then so be it. I won't pressure and compromise myself when it comes to choosing my new home."

Meanwhile, I have widened my search parameters and found a couple of properties to view. I have already made appointments for Saturday.

December 2003

Something interesting has happened. I just had a call from the estate agents. My buyers have withdrawn because they couldn't get a mortgage. I didn't feel the slightest bit unsettled, rather quite relieved because it means some breathing space. I'm still going to see the five properties on Saturday and will make an offer if something really clicks.

☆ ☆ ☆ ☆ ☆ ☆

My goodness! Yet another call from the estate agents – five people are booked on Saturday to view our property. I'm really impressed with their efforts although it helps that the house is a very good deal.

☆ ☆ ☆ ☆ ☆ ☆

Fear continues its hold. Looking at properties not really suitable for me, a little voice keeps whispering "hardly any properties coming onto the market; you may have to compromise". And so I've been doing as I always do when in the grip of fear: twist myself into a pretzel trying to see potential where there is very little.

It's not as if my intuition weren't trying to warn me. After every viewing I'd feel down but unsure exactly why.

Then last Friday, telling someone about my house hunt, I said without thinking. "I haven't seen anything yet that makes my heart beat faster". Hearing the words coming out of my own mouth broke fear's hold on me. No-one was chasing me. The false belief that only once I have my new home will I be able to get on with my life just adds pressure. Stopping to think about it I have genuinely been getting on with my life for the last eight months or so and am doing really well. I just forgot.

My own Truth is often submerged in my fear, which dissipates only when I allow my inner wisdom a voice.

☆ ☆ ☆ ☆ ☆ ☆

Something amazing has happened. I found my new home, a two-bedroom flat in Letchworth Garden City, only a short walk from the station. It has a beautiful feel to it, spacious, light and airy. I felt this sense of "recognition" and a silent 'yes' and a nod that I have only experienced once before. I made an offer there and then.

☆ ☆ ☆ ☆ ☆

As from next week I'll be having twelve days' off work for the Christmas and New Year's break. As the season of good cheer is drawing nearer I feel that eating my meals in my room alone while Jim is downstairs on his own just seems silly. So, yesterday, I suggested a truce, specifically about sharing the shopping, cooking and meals. He agreed. I have no idea if this will work.

☆ ☆ ☆ ☆ ☆

I'm looking at my previous entry and I cannot but shake my head at my pretend self-containment – expressed for my own benefit under the guise that "I'm OK." 'It seems silly', does it? The truth was that I didn't want to be alone.

Now that Christmas is over I admit it was a "going through the motions of pretend companionship". I was uncomfortable sitting with him downstairs and yet I didn't want to be by myself either. I'm relieved to be going back to my routine.

☆ ☆ ☆ ☆ ☆

It's two o'clock in the morning and I've been tossing and turning for the last couple of hours, my mind in turmoil. I'm feeling very, very angry and unbelievably hurt. I have finally decided to stop being so bloody mature and enlightened and I don't fucking want to take responsibility for having been the one who chose him in the first place; I don't fucking want to take responsibility for having stayed with Jim for 37 years so I have decided to end the year with a fucking useless question: How the fuck could I have been with somebody for 30-fucking-7 years without me having made the slightest bit of difference in his life? How can I have mattered so little to him that my presence in his life was so fucking meaningless? How is that possible?!?!

January 2004

I've been feeling completely confused by a sense of, on the one hand, knowing something absolutely and yet, on the other, it's as if I don't know it at all.

For example, one thing I know absolutely is that I matter deeply to myself. The decisions I have taken over the last year are evidence of that. They made me stronger and clearer and have changed the way I live my life, all because I have finally come to see that I do matter. Staying with Jim would have meant continuing to set myself aside. But it would have been even more unforgivable knowing what I was doing to myself. What came out of my mouth when I was telling my friend Gail how hurt I've been feeling because of how little I mattered to Jim tells a different story. Gail noticed and told me, "It sounds to me like you're looking to the outside to give permission to yourself to believe that you matter." I didn't know what to say.

I know absolutely that I will be all right, that I will have a home of my own where I really and truly belong and that financially things will sort themselves out as well. And yet I am still worrying about getting enough for our house.

All this inner confusion and struggle ends in absolute exhaustion. My back pain has returned and on Wednesday evening I lost my voice. I struggled in to work on Thursday and had a sensational selling day, but by the evening I knew staying at home on Friday was a good move. I was virtually immobile and the rest has done me good.

I know I'm doing good things to support myself physically and emotionally, particularly creating opportunities for "me" time. But my body and my emotions are telling me that I need to do more. It's just that I don't know what exactly.

☆ ☆ ☆ ☆ ☆

In a weak moment I asked myself if I had expected too much of Jim. What I was looking for in our relationship was that both of us occasionally put ourselves out for the other. Especially when we see how much it matters to the person who, presumably, we love. We never shared our feelings. We never tried to understand each other. We rarely listened to each other and there was no mutual support when the going got rough. But it wasn't only that. It was about Jim never doing anything for me unless it suited him or in his own good time, if at all. It was about his rejection of me as a person and as a woman. At least that was the way I experienced it and I have no way of knowing if that was what he intended. Probably not, but that doesn't change the way I feel.

Nearly a year has passed since I first started contemplating the possibility of leaving Jim and these thoughts still go round and round in my head, as if I were trying to justify my decision. My friends tell me that this is absolutely natural and that I expect too much of myself to not expect any emotional backlash. Well, expecting too much of myself is one of the things I do rather well.

☆ ☆ ☆ ☆ ☆

These past few days have been revealing and, in parts, disturbing.

My mind went back to the conversation I had with Gail a couple of weeks ago and I remembered something incredibly important. After her Mum died, she went to a workshop about dying and bereavement where she learned about two questions which burn in the minds of those who know they will soon die: "Have I loved well enough?" and "Have I been loved well enough?" And what came out of my mouth without any thought was: "In that case I hope I don't die soon because I certainly haven't loved well enough, nor have I been loved well enough". The 'not having been loved well enough' is absolutely clear to me, all the way down to the depths of my being. The 'not having loved well enough' tells me that my way of loving Jim had clearly included a huge portion of 'non-love' mixed in with my genuine love. If this were not true then we would not be separating.

It was only much later that I thought, 'I have learned a lot about 'loving well' and perhaps one day I will meet somebody to whom I can say 'I love you' without the subtext of 'if' or 'when' or 'but'. For now, I can love myself 'well enough'. That's good enough for me.

☆ ☆ ☆ ☆ ☆ ☆

As I continue my journey it strikes me how much I already knew about what is true and the extent to which I have covered up this Knowing.

I chose Jim because he was so different from Papi. Papi had high expectations of me which felt like a heavy burden, whereas Jim had none. I always felt helpless with Papi because he was highly intellectual and articulate and could always demolish my childish emotional and clumsily expressed arguments. I remember my analogy very clearly. "I used to feel like a puppet with the strings cut, kicking at air and never connecting".

I felt as if I had been punched in the stomach last week when I heard myself describing my continually failing attempts at connecting with Jim "Like a puppet with the strings cut", I said, "I was never able to make a connection." Then I stopped, shocked to the core.

An equally profound insight brought together all the disconnected strands of what I understood about my relationship with Jim into a coherent whole.

His passivity, which I have been describing throughout this book as well as his unresponsiveness, enabled me to project onto him qualities he had never ever had. It gave me an excuse to behave in a critical, manipulative and controlling manner, often expressing myself through temper tantrums which I knew would achieve nothing and then retreating in frustration and resentment.

In fact, Jim has been Jim throughout, never pretending to be anything other than who he was. My sanctifying and demonising him by turn had nothing whatsoever to do with him. The many different approaches I used to relate to him, from my lovey-dovey ways to my current rage and pain – they are all mine. He simply stood there while I kept banging my head over and over again. Of course, his passivity meant that he never challenged me and my distorted ways of trying to relate to him. I, too, never said "Hold on a minute – this is rubbish – I'm leaving".

Well, I am now – both saying it and doing it.

February 2004

Jim and I have found a way of co-existing for the present, but I'm finding this no-man's land – both in terms of physical surroundings and emotional space – very difficult. I remember commenting some months ago that "the future is now". What I meant then was that I was not going to wait for "I will (do/be/have – whatever) when it (whatever "it" may be) happens." The specific example I had in mind then was "I will finally be able to get on with my life when I move into a place of my very own." Well, I have indeed created a little haven in the guest-room, but it's only one room in a whole house and I'm finding it hard being in that house and sharing the same space with Jim. I know it's only temporary but that doesn't change the way I feel about it.

☆ ☆ ☆ ☆ ☆ ☆

Yesterday I finally allowed myself to admit something that I really didn't want to know – the extent to which I sometimes dislike Jim. What makes this admission so distressing is that he didn't do anything that he hasn't done hundreds of times before. This time, however, it became the embodiment of everything that has been wrong between us. Jim is still the same Jim he has always been; perhaps a little more so, because he's no longer under any pressure from me, expecting and demanding that he try harder. Maybe I no longer deceive myself or feel the need to pretend to feel more positive towards him and maintain the facade of a happy marriage; without this self-deception it would all have crumbled years ago. God! How I wish I had let it crumble!

☆ ☆ ☆ ☆ ☆ ☆

Well, it finally happened: someone has made an offer for the house and we have accepted. The downside (if I can call it that) is that they are a cash buyer and the estate agents told us that they're keen to move in so we have to move out. That means that the focus of the pressure has changed – again.

☆ ☆ ☆ ☆ ☆ ☆

I can hardly believe it: **I did it!!!** I found a home of my own!

The minute we accepted the offer on Tuesday I decided that on Saturday I would find a home of my own – that was my unswerving intention – *and I did!*

I'm so thrilled! I just knew this was the right place for me the minute I walked in. It's in Letchworth Garden City, like the other flat I saw before Christmas. Letchworth is 20 minutes north of Welwyn Garden City by train, so it makes the journey to work much longer. But there is a fast train so it's not too bad. It does mean that my annual season ticket will go up by about £700 but, at the same time, the price for this flat is well within my budget.

I love the spacious feel of the place, the fact that I can have friends around for a meal, that I can see trees when I look out of both the bedroom and the living room windows and the kitchen is beautifully appointed.

I made an offer there and then and, after some negotiation, they accepted. This now leaves Jim.

Before setting off this morning the post delivered details of a flat in Welwyn Garden City – well within my budget, so I immediately made an appointment to see it. To my frustration the earliest possible date was Monday evening because the owners wouldn't see anybody over the weekend.

So, having had my offer for the Letchworth flat accepted there was still the viewing in Welwyn Garden City on Monday.

Then I thought I'll meditate on the situation and this made me decide to cancel the appointment. I decided to embrace change whole-heartedly, to start my whole life anew. It was something I had read earlier in the day that led me to this decision and it had to do with sacrifice: "what am I willing to sacrifice to follow my call?" And the answer that came to me was "my life as I'm living it now" – and Welwyn Garden City belongs to that life which is why I'm willing to let it go.

But there is still some important stability in my life – my job, a job I enjoy, am good at and where I'm surrounded by colleagues with good hearts. It's what has kept me going this past year.

March 2004

Over the last couple of weeks I've been putting myself under intense emotional pressure again. I've been feeling deeply sad and crying a lot without really understanding why. Why am I crying and feeling so exhausted all the time when I have finally let go of the lie I've been living all these years? I should be feeling energised.

I've been comparing myself with others: people end relationships all the time and don't make such a meal of it. Deep down, though, I still know that my way to genuine healing lies in honouring all my feelings. Apart from letting myself feel sad, this period is also providing me with rich material for reflection and learning, particularly about how I brought myself both into and out of this place.

Yet again I'm sabotaging myself. As always, I isolate myself and then feel lonely. Not talking with my friends about what's going on is blocking my progress. I'm also out of touch with what's going on with them.

I've identified various mechanisms I use to isolate myself. I tell myself I really don't want to talk to anybody. I play the hero. Why bore them when I can handle it myself? Actually, I can't, not without ending up all alone, with stomach cramps and backache. So, on the spur of the moment, I decided to call John. Although he has left the company, we have stayed in touch. As soon as I decided to phone him I felt myself resisting but made myself call him anyway. I'm not sure why I'm surprised that, as soon as he answered the phone, I burst into tears. As we spoke, the sadness began to evaporate. But the best part was when I dared to admit that I'd been reluctant to call him because I was afraid of being a bore. He just burst out laughing. After a moment of feeling disconcerted, I too burst out laughing. It was absolutely wonderful. We're meeting for a meal next week. I now find it totally incomprehensible that staying in touch used to only mean meeting for a meal, totally forgetting that phones are there for in-between.

It is as if a heavy burden has been lifted from my shoulders. I am so much more at peace.

☆ ☆ ☆ ☆ ☆ ☆

I haven't heard anything from the estate agents about how things are progressing with my flat – my flat! I suppose no news is good news. Anyway, I'm sure they would only call if there was bad news and I can't imagine what bad news there could be in this context. Not long to go!

☆ ☆ ☆ ☆ ☆

More than two weeks later and I'm still feeling strong and at peace. I'm enjoying my job, I'm going out, sometimes on my own, sometimes with a friend, and I enjoy both my solitude and my time with others.

Looking back over the past year, it sounds as if I'm going backwards and forwards – I'm happy/I'm sad, I'm confused/I'm clear, I'm angry/I'm at peace, I feel loved/I feel lonely. In exploring this I notice two things. I'm happier longer than I'm sad, I'm clear longer than I'm confused, I'm at peace longer than I'm angry and I feel loved longer than I feel lonely. I also know something else: *this* is how life is, rich in laughter and tears, sorrow and joy – and that's what makes it all so full and rewarding.

Even without such a life-changing experience, living is not a tidy process. I'm learning to express what I'm truly feeling at any one time, with no pressure to justify or even understand why I feel the way I do. It's equally clear that I forget this from time to time but, I believe it is more important to note that I am remembering more often than forgetting.

Jim, too, is about to start his life-change. He told me yesterday that he has decided to move to another country. From the moment he told me of his plans I knew this was absolutely right for him and feel really excited on his behalf.

☆ ☆ ☆ ☆ ☆

Another week has elapsed since my last observations and I'm still feeling deeply happy and at peace. In fact, yesterday I turned 59 and I had a great time. In my company, it is part of the culture that birthdays be marked with some drinks and nibbles, a card signed by all and about 15 minutes or so for a get-together. In the past, this seemed like routine but yesterday I felt deeply moved. The genuine affection of my colleagues meant it was a very special time for me. Mentioning this to Mami afterwards she suggested that it's because I am now authentic myself. Maybe I had been the one to treat it as a ritual. That thought made me pause. I actually hadn't made the connection.

At 59 I feel powerful and strong. It's an incredibly exciting time for me and, even better, I'm feeling all these things **now**.

April 2004

The past week has been an absolute revelation.

Two weeks ago my estate agent alerted me that, although the offer on our property was made and accepted more than seven weeks ago, no progress whatsoever has been made on our buyer's side. No survey has been arranged nor fees paid to their solicitor to get searches underway. They, therefore, strongly recommended I reconsider my options, which is code for putting the house back on the market. I told them that I would much rather wait another week before starting all over again and then probably go through another three months of viewing. I just couldn't bear it.

After a further exchange with my estate agent I suddenly realised that I was acting out of fear. I called them and instructed them to call our buyer and tell them that they had two working days to get a survey organised; after that the house would go back on the market. Two days later we still hadn't heard so on Wednesday I gave our estate agents the go-ahead. And, what's best, I feel no anxiety whatsoever.

It is very likely that, as a result, I might lose my own flat where everything has been progressing so smoothly. However, ever since that moment when I let go of the fear (or the fear let go of me) I've been feeling totally at peace, knowing that everything will be all right in the end. I simply have to accept that at this stage, I don't know what "all right" might look like.

☆ ☆ ☆ ☆ ☆ ☆

I got a phone call from our estate agents today, three days after my last comments. An appointment has been made with the buyer's surveyor for this coming week.

☆ ☆ ☆ ☆ ☆ ☆

Something really interesting happened to me last Monday: I lost the flat I was planning to buy. The estate agent called to say that the seller decided not to sell after all, because his personal circumstances had changed. What I find extraordinary is my reaction, as if I had been given good news and the strongest sense of relief. How bizarre is that!

The way reality looks right now is that the sale of our house is going ahead and I have nowhere to go – and that's absolutely all right with me.

I would go further: I feel as if I have undergone a deeply fundamental change in the last couple of weeks, which I find hard to describe. Instead of being afraid of all the things that may or may not happen, I'm feeling incredibly happy, at peace and excited about the future.

I've decided that I really don't want to live in Letchworth nor, to my amazement, in Welwyn Garden City. I have no idea where that leaves me but that's all right too. What I will do is find an unfurnished flat to rent for a while, until I find a place "that makes my heart beat faster." I like the sound of that. A place "that makes my heart beat faster."

Right now, that's all I know and that's more than enough for me.

May 2004

It's only a month since I finished writing the previous paragraph and again I feel like exclaiming "this is so unlike me!" Ever since I was told that the flat I chose as my new home was not going to happen; ever since I decided to rent to allow time to find a home that would "make my heart beat faster"; ever since I entered into a state of total uncertainty – I've been mostly feeling incredibly happy.

My external experiences are challenging. Financially, the dream of having a home of my own seems to be receding very fast indeed, because both interest rates and house prices are rising. In addition, my plan to rent means two removal expenses instead of one and I had forgotten the stamp duty. Despite all my efforts, I still haven't found a place to rent that is unfurnished, so I don't have to pay additional storage expenses.

But there is an interesting and significant inner shift: I'm detaching myself from my expectations and what my situation "should look like".

Finding a suitable place is taking longer than I expected (there's that word again – 'expected') and the buyer of our house has started making noises about wanting to move in. Enter Plan C. This involves taking a room in somebody's house for a few weeks and putting my belongings into storage. I have no idea if that is even possible.

Meanwhile, my friend John whom I met for dinner yesterday made a casual comment.

"I can really see you", he said, "on a house boat." My jaw is still on the floor at this off-the-wall idea. But, as outrageous and "so unlike me" as it sounded, what's even more uncharacteristic is that I haven't dismissed it out of hand. I will look into it. I find myself in a situation of the unknown which only a few short years ago would send me into a spin of anxiety and fear, and I'm experiencing a degree of uncertainty which used to paralyse me with terror and wake me at 2:00 or 3:00 in the morning just staring into the darkness unable to go back to sleep again. Instead, I'm feeling happy and excited, looking forward to whatever Life is planning for me next.

Tomorrow is Saturday and I have a couple of places to see that I might rent.

I can't believe it! I'm on my way home – just hours after I recorded my previous reflections. I have actually found the perfect place. It is within easy access to public transport, surrounded by trees and lots of green, and I can hear bird song which I love. The kitchen is beautiful with everything I could possibly need or want and the double bedroom with a wall-to-wall fitted wardrobe is light and airy. A small parade of shops is a minute's walk away. It also has a garage (storage space!!!) and, what to me is nothing less than a miracle, the monthly rent has been reduced by £175 and is within my reach.

The situation had become critical: our buyer wanted to know if she could move in by the end of the month (less than three weeks away), which sent me, briefly, into a spin of panic. Once my head had cleared I asked myself what else I could do to find a place to rent. There is an expression "to cast your bread across the waters" which I completed in my head "and see what comes back."

Who could I approach for help? Instead of falling back on old friends, two women I had recently met at a one-day workshop came to mind. I had hit it off straight away with Ros and Andrea. I sent both an email explaining my situation, the challenge of my limited budget and my immediate need for somewhere to live.

Ros replied saying she had a room in her own house she planned to rent out. Andrea put me in touch with a friend of hers, Gerlinde, who sounded very kind and understanding having undergone a similar experience to mine – separating from a long term relationship and having to find a place of her own – several years ago. Since then she had become a relocation specialist. She called me back a couple of hours later pointing me in the direction of the flat I have just described.

I can hardly wait until tomorrow to call and tell her what happened – that, and put the wheels in motion for the next stage of my life to begin.

It's only a week later and, having been at the receiving end of even more blessings,

I went into a downward spin. The thoughts were overwhelming. "This is too much", "this is more than I can handle", "I'm not ready for all this!". I was feeling as if I'd been overdoing a banquet – too much of all the goodies available: love, support, a beautiful (if temporary) new home, a gorgeous setting and then saying to myself "this is more than I can handle".

My interpretation of my feelings as a "downward spin" implies something negative, judging the feeling to be bad rather than potentially useful information. When I do this, I put an unnecessary emotional burden on myself. The useful information I should be reading is "I have enough on my plate to be getting on with" and take it from there.

Phone calls from our solicitors and the estate agents let me know that contracts have been exchanged and completion is Friday, 4 June 2004. Jim's flight is scheduled for the 8th so he will spend the days in between at my flat. "My flat" – it has a great ring!

Despite all this progress my body is hurting (backache, headaches, no energy) and I feel very sad. A long process is coming to an end. Realising that I have to leave Jim, telling him last June and then going through the process involved an enormous amount of grieving, learning and growing. I only hope that I can handle the coming three weeks with as much strength and love.

☆ ☆ ☆ ☆ ☆ ☆

Well, there go my hopes of a fairly graceful conclusion to the process. Yesterday, as Jim was being Jim – I absolutely lost it, for the first time in this past year I really, really lost it. It's a wonder I didn't murder him. That's not all. I said some awful things to him and, even worse, I don't regret it one little bit. After I finished hyper-ventilating and shaking and crying and screaming at him, I looked back at what had happened. Even in my worst temper tantrums over the years I've always been careful not to say things that I might regret later. I maintained a tight control over my true feelings. Not this Saturday. Astonishingly, I have no regrets. In fact, afterwards, I felt giddy from the experience. That raises important questions about healthy expression of anger. Suppressing angry feelings is clearly not an option but expressing feelings which, though absolutely true are deeply hurtful if not destructive, surely that can't be an option either?

☆ ☆ ☆ ☆ ☆ ☆

Since I recorded the above yesterday, I wonder if perhaps the main issue is not letting it get to this stage. As Alan told me a couple of years ago, If I'd expressed my true feelings as I was experiencing them I wouldn't have reached a stage where I was practically ready to explode and turn everything around me into rubble – except, of course, that it didn't. I don't know how anybody else would have felt at the receiving end of my explosion but Jim seemed only mildly concerned. He came to me later and said he didn't mean to upset me. So I explained that the incident which had caused my reaction was just one of the reasons we arrived at the point we have. I told him how deeply tired I was and he suggested – as he often has in the past – that it is my lifestyle which is the cause for my tiredness – because I get up very early. But this time I made it absolutely clear that it is not my lifestyle that's affecting me but the relationship.

"It's about you and me", I said, "not my lifestyle – "YOU (pause) and ME".

But I know he doesn't understand. I could see it in his face.

Not that it matters. I've been building up to this. In the last week or so feelings of anger and pain have mounted. I accept these as part of the process but not once in this past year have I told Jim what my true feelings were, mainly because I thought I'd already said everything I had to say. Clearly I had more to say and, on Saturday, I did.

☆ ☆ ☆ ☆ ☆ ☆

About six weeks ago, before I found the flat, I enrolled on a very special three day workshop called "Spiritual Renewal". I have gradually become aware that I'm reaching a stage in my life where my spiritual development is important to me. It seemed vital to me to experience the event, even if I couldn't say exactly why.

As I booked it I knew that the timing was likely to be awkward because of the house move. I was right. It's only one week before D-day and just ten days before Jim finally exits from my life. Although awkward at one level, on another the timing is nothing short of perfect. It marks the end of an eighteen month long painful, yet rewarding, process and the beginning of a new stage in my life. As it turned out, the event itself was transformational.

Over the period leading up to the workshop there had been no let-up in my feelings of pain and anger. The need for relief increased my longing for the workshop to take place.

Booking that workshop was one of the best decisions I ever made. I was instantly, profoundly aware of being surrounded by people in pain, feeling alone, having experienced terrible betrayals and abuse. Yet, despite it all these people wanted to connect with something greater than themselves. Like me, they just didn't know how to do this. I made a genuinely warm connection with three people and spent time together with them during breaks. Particularly beautiful was sharing the laughter. It has been a very long time since I last laughed so much and so deeply from my belly. It felt like being able to breathe again.

But it was the workshop itself that produced nothing less than a miracle. One of the exercises involved each one of us taking it in turns to sit in the "hot seat". We were called at random. That person had to say why they were there and then was offered a bowl full of folded pieces of paper, each representing a message meant just for them.

My turn came on day 2. I'm sitting in the "hot seat" trying to explain what brought me to this workshop. Then Miranda (Miranda Holden, the workshop leader) held out the bowl and asked me to pick one of the pieces of paper. When I opened it my reaction was "Oh shit! No! I can't do that! I'm not ready!" I burst into heartbroken sobs, pouring out all my pain and anger – both towards Jim and also towards myself. The piece of paper said "Embrace forgiveness".

Finally, when I had recovered, Miranda spoke to me soothingly. I can't remember what she said. What I do remember is finally getting to a place – one that I've reached many times before – the one that says "I don't want this anymore. I surrender." I recognise this place as the point where transformation can occur. But this was so big for me that, although I was willing, I really didn't believe it would actually happen. Before guiding us through a forgiveness meditation, she asked us, 'who do we choose to forgive?' I chose myself and, when she prompted me to be more specific, I felt my Shadow emerge and I chose the part of me that I regarded as unworthy of love. As this came unthinkingly out of my mouth I was initially shocked and then realised it was true or I wouldn't have stayed with Jim for 37 years.

My whole body started shaking, then my head felt very hot for a while and I even sobbed a little but, when it was all over, all my anger and pain had disappeared. In its place was an extraordinary feeling of peace and joy.

Over the last few months I had noticed that, when I spoke to Jim, my voice was sharp, my eyes cold and I could feel a physical sensation that felt like my heart snapping shut. It was a horrible feeling. Now, on my way back from day 2 of the workshop I wondered how I would feel when I looked at Jim (after all, he was not the object of my forgiveness; I was).

When I got home it was absolutely wonderful to find that I was able to look at him with a feeling of tenderness and softness. And the feeling still persists. Such an intense sense of relief, a feeling of a heavy burden having been lifted and I am deeply at peace.

Since then I've been reflecting on what I learned on this workshop, particularly on how to approach the challenges that life sends me. Undeniably, I have made genuine progress over the last few years towards shedding my false beliefs and the multiple layers of self deception. It often felt as if I had to invoke a lot of strength, courage and persistence to do so. I think I've made it such hard work because I've been trying to do it all by myself. I don't want to do it alone anymore, nor have to struggle every inch of the way. I want to learn to let go and be able to surrender to a Higher Being. I need to know that I don't have to keep on struggling by myself, rather, to be able to just allow myself to be and to know that I will be all right.

June 2004

Well, it's all over. Today, 9 June 2004, I've come to work really early to record my feelings and I'm finding it incredibly hard. I can't believe how distressed I am.

The last few days have been so strange. Jim and I worked extremely hard and very well together throughout the moving process – out of the old place and into the new one.

Ever since that weekend with Miranda everything changed between us. Not only have I found an inner peace but the old tenderness is back between Jim and I, without it meaning anything other than that.

By the time the flat was in a liveable state it was quite late. Jim and I flopped on the settee, totally exhausted. We just sat there for a while. His expression changed and he looked at me with a question in his eyes. I opened my arms we held each other in silence, needing no words.

He was scheduled to fly off yesterday, 8 June 2004, and as late as the day before

I still wasn't sure whether I wanted to come to work as usual or see him off. It was important to me that, whatever I chose, it would be because that's what I really wanted to do. I only decided the previous evening that I really did want to see him off. Now I'm glad I did.

He was flying out of Gatwick and I went with him as far as Clapham Junction where we had time to have coffee together. I felt I needed to explain – again – why we were actually here. I reiterated that I wasn't sure if he actually understood why we had arrived this far, but I loved him and always would. I also added that I'd done my utmost to make it work. I know he still didn't understand because, as far as he's concerned, I was "throwing it all away" (as he told me more than once over the past year) and, to him, that didn't make sense. I knew he wouldn't but it was important to me to say it once more and so I did.

Then it was time for him to leave. As we got up, I said, "I'm feeling numb" and then, a moment later, I burst into tears.

"I don't feel numb at all", I said, "I feel very sad". Then we hugged and he left – and that was that. I couldn't stop crying even though I didn't doubt for a single moment that I made the right decision. But that doesn't make any difference to how I'm feeling.

☆ ☆ ☆ ☆ ☆

I'm now living in Ham, a suburb of Richmond. The first few days I worried that I might accidentally end up back in Welwyn Garden City when I left work to go home so I made a note to myself which I stuck on my computer screen: "Home is Ham." It makes me smile.

I've now been alone in my new home for two days – or evenings, to be precise. It's beginning to take shape and looks really nice. But I'm not there yet. I'm looking forward to this weekend. I'm planning to do a lot of cleaning. I also want to go into Richmond, get things for the flat and explore the area. On Sunday I want to look around my new neighbourhood.

☆ ☆ ☆ ☆ ☆

The people in the other flats are very kind and helpful, giving me information and doing small things to smooth my path, not knowing my way around yet.

☆ ☆ ☆ ☆ ☆

This is the most amazingly beautiful area. I can't believe how perfect it is. I have to smile at myself because, when I still had nowhere to live I kept praying continuously for a new home in Welwyn Garden City. In fact, I had very precise specifications. I'm learning that God knows better. That's the control freak in me, the one I'm trying to let go – obviously not always successfully.

This past week felt odd. The weather has been radiantly sunny, everything around here's so beautiful, the flat is looking really welcoming – yet nothing seemed to touch me. The only thing I've been really conscious of is feeling totally exhausted. Then, these last couple of days I started feeling again – mostly deeply sad and spent several days hiding away, sobbing. In many ways I felt relieved. Feeling numb is quite unpleasant, like being frozen and detached from life.

Alan commented, "I'm not surprised you're so exhausted; it's been a very long and difficult year." He also suggested I regard this state as being jet-lagged and give myself time to recover both physically and emotionally.

☆ ☆ ☆ ☆ ☆ ☆

I've had a great weekend. I suddenly had a sense of "having arrived". I saw clearly that I've achieved what I set out to do. I made a commitment to myself and kept it, through thick and thin. I kept faith with myself and I now know, in a way I never knew before, that I can truly trust myself.

On the practical side, I took a bus into town – went to the cinema, bought yet more things for the flat, the best of which was a very large plant which looks perfect in its chosen spot.

Tomorrow, Saturday, 26 June, I have Toria and her partner, Jol coming over. They're helping out with bits and bobs and I'm going to cook them a meal. And, on Sunday, Ros is coming over just for us to spend some time together. I will cook for her as well.

What makes all this so special is that I've never cooked for friends before, at least not a proper meal. Cooking was Jim's department but in the last eighteen months I didn't want anybody coming to the house. It didn't feel like my home anymore and I'd always meet friends at restaurants.

This feels really good.

July 2004

On Friday Andrew, my manager, asked me when was the last time I took time off just to relax and I realised that it has been over two years. So, on the spur of the moment, I decided to take five days off which, with two weekends tacked at both ends actually makes it nine days. That's from 24 July.

Ever since I made up my mind to do this I've been feeling quite vulnerable about the whole idea. I've never taken a long break on my own before. I have no idea what to do with all this time.

I called my friend Niki yesterday and told her about my plans and she immediately asked me to stay with them for a couple of days. We haven't seen each other for months – ever since she moved away from Welwyn Garden City – so I'm thrilled with the idea. We used to meet almost weekly but, since they moved to Huntingdon, spending time together has become a treat.

Am I pushing myself before I'm ready to move onto the next stage of my life? Perhaps I am in avoidance. It's true that I have been in my (temporary) flat for only two weeks and it's equally true that I'm still feeling jet-lagged. How do I know I'm still jet-lagged? I don't feel at all ready to move on. I feel I just want to regroup. I guess I'm answering my own question.

What brought this train of thought about is that I've identified potentially affordable areas for buying a flat, only to find that I really don't want to go and look at any of them.

Everything in me cries out "It's too soon! I'm not ready!" It's just that I don't want to avoid doing what I know needs to be done, but how will I know when I'm ready?

It's only a few days after my last entry and I'm beginning to emerge from my jet-lag stage. In fact, I'm feeling terrific.

☆ ☆ ☆ ☆ ☆ ☆

It's just a month since I wrote the previous paragraph and again I feel like exclaiming "this is so unlike me!" Even though externally my experience resembles a roller-coaster ride, I mostly feel incredibly happy and deeply at peace. I think I'm ready to move to the next stage of my life.

☆ ☆ ☆ ☆ ☆ ☆

I'm struck by the extent to which I delight in living on my own. I can't believe how wonderful it feels. I'm experiencing a deep sense of peace and intense pleasure. I particularly enjoy the silence – sitting on the settee and gazing at the trees or doing things around the flat. Quite by accident, I found a lovely park nearby, with benches facing a little pond full of ducks and swans and very few people around. This is amazing. All I can say is that I'm truly blessed.

☆ ☆ ☆ ☆ ☆ ☆

I'm having a completely new experience that is causing me intense pain and has to do, of all things, with expressing love for another human being. I've met an old man who is homeless yet choosing to deal with it in his own way. This means he won't let me help and only rarely lets me buy him a packet of biscuits.

"I'm homeless", he points out uncompromisingly, "not a beggar".

The problem is that I'm still trying to fix and rescue and that's part of my struggle.

I have come to realise that loving people my way is actually less for their benefit than for mine. I'm finding it incredibly hard to just be there for this man in the way he needs and wants. I have to check with him before I can even buy him a cup of coffee. Sometimes he lets me, sometimes not. What matters most to him, he tells me, is to be able to return the kindness by buying me the occasional pack of biscuits or cup of coffee.

I don't see him as a homeless person. To me, he's Gerry, an old man who happens to be homeless, which is very different.

This kind of loving – letting the other person be – is far beyond my comfort zone. I always believed I knew how to make a difference. Finding that my way of loving is not wanted confuses me. How else can I express love?

☆ ☆ ☆ ☆ ☆ ☆

My current reflections have been brewing for some weeks now.

It all started with Helen, a woman I met at a workshop. I tend to feel uncomfortable in large groups of strangers so, at the break I had intended to follow my habit of looking out of the window pretending to find the view absolutely fascinating in order not to have to just stand there and start some inane conversation with a stranger.

This time, however, Helen turned to me.

"Would you like a glass of water?", she asked. I jumped up. "Yes, please", I said, "I'll come along with you." When we returned to our seat she introduced me to her friend Ros who was talking to Andrea, the Ros and Andrea I remained in touch with – Helen went back to the Midlands.

Amazingly, it turns out that Andrea lives less than ten minutes away from my flat. I have already mentioned that it was she who indirectly pointed me to my new home.

But recently my thoughts keep returning to Helen whose only role seems to have been to bring Ros and Andrea into my life. In fact, Helen didn't do anything extraordinary; she was just being Helen – thoughtful and kind – and this is why her simple action is having such an intense effect on me.

I know she has no idea of the extent to which she impacted on my life just as I don't know how I impact on the life of others or, for that matter, how everybody affects everybody else. That's why love, kindness, thoughtfulness, truthfulness and integrity are so important – we can change the world in ways we cannot even begin to imagine.

☆ ☆ ☆ ☆ ☆ ☆

I think the time has come for me to start looking for a permanent place of my own. I'm very conscious that it's already end of July and I'm only renting this flat for 6 months. It could have been for longer but at the time I was conscious of having to fully repay my mortgage by the time I retire in nine years. OK, come Monday, I'll start looking in earnest.

☆ ☆ ☆ ☆ ☆ ☆

Quite by accident, I discovered that one possible answer to the housing question is a shared ownership scheme under the auspices of the Richmond Housing Trust. My personal circumstances meet their criteria for inclusion on their waiting list. It could be quite a long wait and, in fact, they stressed that some people have been waiting for over two years so I know that I can't count on this. I still have to look for other options.

☆ ☆ ☆ ☆ ☆ ☆

I can't believe this! A letter from the Housing Trust came yesterday, Saturday, advising me that a new development with three two-bedroom flats had become available in Richmond – not far from my where I am living.

They are holding an open day on Thursday, 5 August for people on their list. I called them for directions and to check it was OK if I came after work. They warned me that the flats were going on a first-come-first-served basis so, by the evening it was highly likely the flats would be gone. I now plan to arrive a little before opening time.

August 2004

I arrived at the block of flats a few minutes before opening time – only to find that three other people had had the same idea and one of the three flats had already been claimed.

I joined the queue and was given a slip – No. 4, just like at a delicatessen.

I viewed the remaining two – with my eyes popping out of their sockets: the spaciousness, the luxury, the fitted kitchen, fitted carpets throughout. Both flats were absolutely amazing. One had slightly larger rooms but the other, although the rooms were slightly smaller, actually "made my heart sing". What made the difference was being able to see trees from every window. It was breathtaking. I put my name down immediately and instantly felt as if the flat was already mine. However, the woman explained that she was unable to confirm; she would first need to check her records. That was on the Tuesday. On the Friday evening I found a voicemail message telling me that they would let me know one way or the other "sometime next week".

It's now Thursday, 9 August and I still haven't heard whether or not the flat has been allocated to me. I try to keep hold of my deep belief that I'm meant to be in this flat and wanting it desperately while, at the same time, trying to relax, knowing that somehow things will work out all right – with the subtext that it couldn't possibly be "all right" for me not to have this flat.

I was exhausted by all this pulling myself apart until I finally shouted inside my head *"stop! I don't want to do this to myself anymore!"*

Then, this morning, I felt an inner shift taking place during my meditation practice. I had remembered that, for the last six months, if not longer, I've been praying regularly for "a home where I really and truly belong, that will support who I am and who I am in the process of becoming." Then a question came to me: "How do you know that this flat would actually support you in this? Are you saying you know what the Grand Scheme is?" For all I know, this flat, although to my mind absolutely perfect, might actually turn out not to be in my best interests. The point is, I don't know. It's about surrendering control to God, as Miranda Holden had said all those months ago at her workshop. I know that when I do relinquish control, I become open to all kinds of possibilities, often things that hadn't occurred to me before. That, plus the intense feeling of relief of letting go of my belief about how things should turn out – what's best for me and what isn't.

☆ ☆ ☆ ☆ ☆ ☆

It's early morning, the next day. A voicemail message from the Housing Trust tells me that I did *not* get the flat. Apparently, someone else had a prior claim from an earlier viewing.

Despite everything I said yesterday I'm experiencing a deep sense of loss. A question keeps ringing in my head, "Now what, God?" Deep down, I really did believe that I was meant to be there; it felt so right. I don't want to go back to checking websites, listing possible locations and generally rushing around in a panic of frenzied activity. This time I feel the need to stay with my disappointment and loss, at least for a little while. I also want to talk about how I'm feeling with Ros and Andrea, both of whom I feel closest to. I need their emotional support to help me clear out my fears and beliefs about having to compromise, move miles and miles away because I can't afford anything closer to my work in London and all the ways I put myself through the wringer. At the same time, I also need space to gather myself together because I really don't know what to do next. The one thing I do notice, though, is that, although I'm feeling sad, I'm not actually feeling scared.

☆ ☆ ☆ ☆ ☆ ☆

I've told one or two of my colleagues at work about losing the flat and I'm noticing how uncomfortable people are with feelings of sadness and disappointment. One commented, "Oh, well, never mind. You'll bounce back soon enough."

My reply was, "I will, but not yet. Right now I'm feeling really sad and disappointed."

I no longer pretend to feel upbeat and cheerful to "protect" people from their own feelings of discomfort – or to conceal my vulnerability.

☆ ☆ ☆ ☆ ☆ ☆

Strange as it may seem, it's only been two days and already I feel as if I'm fully "back." Both Ros and Andrea have been a great source of strength. It's important that neither of them colluded with my "poor little me" drama. A few minutes of "what a shame" and "you must be feeling really disappointed", helped me feel validated and was followed by "keep an open mind – the right place is there – just waiting for you." I'm sure they're right.

☆ ☆ ☆ ☆ ☆ ☆

OK, I've had enough of being self-indulgent. I've been wallowing for over a week now. It's time for me to start looking for a place to live. I really can't go on like this.

The problem is that I don't know *where* to look. I can find places on a map but the names mean nothing to me. I believe I should focus on a specific area and, since I don't know what area that should be, I feel unable to take any action.

Since today is Sunday and I'm taking a day off work tomorrow, I decided it's alright to stay in this state of paralysis just a little while longer – say until Tuesday.

☆ ☆ ☆ ☆ ☆ ☆

Today has been exhausting and challenging. Only now, as I'm on my way home can I look back on it with some degree of clarity and understanding.

When the shared ownership flat fell through I was confronted with the fact that I only have 3½ months left before my rental agreement ends and I felt paralysed, not knowing how to proceed. I started noticing a tight, slightly sick feeling around my stomach indicating that I was beginning to feel anxious. This anxiety exploded into the most intense fear at the end of my lunch break, which I had spent on the internet trying to make appointments to view flats on Saturday.

I spent the last couple of hours after work with Alan.

It's such a relief to be able to share with him what I'm currently experiencing and, as always, I came away in a completely different, clearer and lighter frame of mind.

None of it is new. What it boils down to is the extent to which fear clouds my judgement, limits my creativity and narrows my options.

Although I knew that fear does this to me I felt completely gripped by it. Alan reminded me that I've lived in fear for most of my adult life and that revisiting that fear is normal. Then he commented "You make fear real by attaching a 'because' to whatever you're dealing with at any particular time", and he added, "The reality is that, on the one hand, you feel fear and, on the other, you have a problem that needs to be solved. The two are unrelated. The fear has always been within you and will find a focus, whatever the issue".

He's right, of course. I suddenly became conscious of a belief I didn't know I held, namely that all the blessings I've been showered with have been flukes and the challenges and disappointments are the reality when it's the other way round. It is the disappointments that are the bleeps, not the blessings.

I'm going to try a different way of finding a place to live, although, as yet I have no idea what that would be.

☆ ☆ ☆ ☆ ☆

I have organised five appointments for flats to view today. I really don't have a lot of time left so I have to get on with it. Not that I'm putting myself under any pressure, of course.

Will any of the flats make my heart beat faster? It's possible though somewhat unlikely. Does it matter? I've started wondering if it's not what I find that matters – within certain parameters, of course – but rather what I can create with that space.

☆ ☆ ☆ ☆ ☆

This past week has been particularly challenging. I put myself under such heavy pressure, both emotionally and physically, that I was practically on my knees. I might still be there if Ros hadn't noticed and pointed out what I was doing to myself.

Then I noticed that I had begun to allow in thoughts such as "Oh, my God, I left it too late", and "This place is not too bad" when it was clearly unsuitable. I began to feel overwhelmed with fear again and was spending every free moment focusing on finding a flat: every lunchtime I was on the internet and making appointments with estate agents. Then, every evening I was out looking at flats, each one more disheartening than the last. Every spare minute in between, I worried about finding a place to live. And all that on top of carrying out my job. I was literally painting myself into a corner and I simply didn't know how to handle the situation.

And then I finally remembered what was really true, namely that there's no need to be afraid; that I'm loved and supported and that life will send me what's best for me. I don't have any evidence of this other than past experience, but I just know it's true.

☆ ☆ ☆ ☆ ☆

I had lunch with my friend John. My friendship with him is different from Ros and Andrea because he and I go back a very long time.

He's been witnessing my journey from before I even started it in earnest and recognised my current situation as one more stage along the line. He also remembers the process I tend to go through from feeling stuck and fearful, all the way to the other side – and that when I experience strength and clarity, new avenues tend to open up that I hadn't seen when I was swallowed up by fear. What's special about having a friend like John, who has known me for so long, is that he has the clarity I lack when I'm in the middle of life's turbulence. Our conversation over lunch was a reminder of the process and somehow it helped me "to come back to myself". He commented that my whole 'presence' had changed from when I first arrived at the restaurant from 'cowed' (his word) to light, strong and clear. He was right. I could feel it in my body. The physical sensation of strength, lightness and clarity were absolutely unmistakable.

☆ ☆ ☆ ☆ ☆ ☆

I can't believe what has happened. I had only just arrived back at the office after lunch with John when the Housing Trust called. Although it feels like a long time ago, it's only been four weeks since I was told that someone else had priority over the flat I had wanted so badly.

"The reason I'm calling", the woman said, "was to let you know that one of the flats has become available again and, since you're next on the list (so that's what those delicatessen slips were for!) I wondered if you'd like to have a look at it."

Well, my heart and my breathing both seemed to stop. When I recovered, I squeaked, "Yes, please". So, I'm going next Tuesday. I know it's five days away but it's the earliest she could manage.

Despite everything I know and all I have experienced, I still sometimes have a hard time accepting that life is full of wonderful things.

☆ ☆ ☆ ☆ ☆ ☆

It's evening and I have time to review all that has happened today. The sequence of events is just so striking: The lunch with John ending with an inner shift which, in turn, was followed by the phone call from the Housing Trust. It was not the call that caused the inner shift and I wonder if the call came *as a result of* my inner shift?

It sounds bizarre, I know, but the timing is just so amazing.

☆ ☆ ☆ ☆ ☆ ☆

I went to see the flat yesterday and it was just as I remembered it: wonderfully spacious and a view of trees from all the windows. I knew I could be really happy there. All I had dreamed of but better. For a moment I wondered if this was indeed a dream and I would soon wake up. I also wondered how come the flat had become available again.

Then I started worrying.

"What went wrong for the other person?" I asked the woman from the Housing Trust, "Did they not meet some criteria of yours?"

She assured me that it had had nothing to do with the Housing Trust.

"The mortgage provider turned down their application for a mortgage."

"What a bummer", I commented, not entirely sincerely, because I was so thrilled to have a second chance.

Back home I felt so overwhelmed at being at the receiving end of something so special that I got drunk. Not very spiritual, but what the hell.

It took me a couple of hours to arrive at a sense of peace and of – how do I put it – rightness. Not exhilaration, relief or excitement but this by now familiar quiet sense of 'yes' within me.

As I'm recording this I remember how I came to live in Richmond. It has all come together so smoothly and harmoniously. I knew when I first saw the Housing Trust flat all those weeks ago that I belonged there – only to be told that someone else got there first. That didn't feel right. And here I am again, just four weeks and a lifetime later. I find it really hard to believe.

☆ ☆ ☆ ☆ ☆ ☆

I can't understand what's happening to me. One of my colleagues is about to celebrate one of the "big" birthdays (his thirtieth) and is behaving as if he were about to turn a hundred. So I said in a cheerful tone of voice "What are you on about! Next year I'm having my big one!" I suddenly stopped, overwhelmed by the most intense and unexpected feeling of vulnerability which surprised me because my age has always been a big joke to me; it always felt as if it had nothing to do with who I am: I don't look it, I don't feel it and I certainly don't act my age – whatever that's supposed to mean.

My life has changed beyond measure in the last eighteen months and especially in the last four. I'm happy. I'm free. I feel as if a weight has fallen off my shoulders. I feel at peace. My future looks exciting. And yet, right now, none of it changes the way I feel. For one thing, sixty sounds so old. The thought that came to me was "I'm entering the last lap of my life" even though what I'm actually entering is a new beginning.

There was also another thought that pushed its way into my consciousness. Now that I'm growing old, will I ever find love again?

☆ ☆ ☆ ☆ ☆ ☆

I'm sitting on a bench on Richmond Green. I have just been to collect a special delivery letter from the Post Office. I knew it was from the Housing Trust. I hesitated for a moment before opening it. What if I had got the whole thing wrong? What if someone else has a prior claim? But no – there was no mistake: the flat is mine, if I want it (if I want it?!?!) Tears came to my eyes. My prayers had been answered: a home where I really and truly belong. A home that makes my heart sing. Thank you, God.

☆ ☆ ☆ ☆ ☆ ☆

Here I go again. I can't remember the last time I felt so stressed out and absolutely overwhelmed with fear. Was it last week?

The letter from the Housing Trust indicated that contracts have to be exchanged in as little as four weeks. My solicitor believes this may be overly optimistic. I felt so sure that I could come to some arrangement with the Housing Trust because my tenancy agreement at my flat in Ham runs for another three months.

This morning I spoke to the woman at the Trust and explained the situation. I told her I'd be more than happy to get the process going to exchange of contracts, but could they be flexible about the completion date? She had to check, she said. A few minutes ago I found a voicemail message saying that the answer was "no". Either I meet their conditions or the flat will be offered to the next person on the list.

I was stunned. I called my landlady to see if there was some way I might be released earlier, otherwise I would have to pay two months rent as well as the mortgage which would deplete most of my savings. She promised to talk it through with the estate agent, find out what the legal implications were and then call me back.

For some reason I feel confident that it will be alright.

☆ ☆ ☆ ☆ ☆ ☆

My landlady has called me back and explained the options. It turns out that the worst case scenario is I have to pay one month's rent and not two as I'd feared. Anyway, at the end of the day, it's only money – and I will have my home.

☆ ☆ ☆ ☆ ☆ ☆

More welcome news: Today's value of my investments is considerably more than the last quote only two months ago. That means the pressure has been lifted off my shoulders. Oh, my Goodness!

☆ ☆ ☆ ☆ ☆ ☆

The psychological and mental challenges of the past week translated themselves into pain of various degrees of intensity. No matter how much sleep I get, I am still feeling extremely tired. Both could be due to stress. It's only 27 days to the move and everything appears to be rolling along.

I'm saying "appears" because I don't know how the solicitor's side is progressing although I expect they'd let me know if they hit any snags.

Soon this stage in the process will be over and then I will have my new home – the one that makes my heart beat faster and where I really and truly belong (this is my mantra which I keep repeating to myself, because it puts everything in perspective.)

What I do notice is that, despite the exhaustion and all the aches, pains and cramps, I'm actually feeling very happy and peaceful.

☆ ☆ ☆ ☆ ☆ ☆

Well, my emotional state has changed yet again – perhaps not surprisingly.

Even though everything is going really well I'm feeling weepie. What I forget is that, even though I'm incredibly well organised considering that I've never moved home all by myself, it's still unsettling and emotionally draining.

I can't believe I've only been living on my own for four months. It feels like forever. Perhaps, at some level, I've always lived on my own. This thought could clear up another puzzle.

I feel as if I've never been married. I don't feel like a woman who has separated from her husband after 37 years' marriage. It is as if it had never happened. It must have a lot to do with my definition of being married: sharing one's life, both caring about each other's well-being as well as one's own and being genuinely interested in each other.

All that and much, much more. That's the way I imagine a genuinely loving marriage.

I can't imagine why I'm even thinking about all this, especially when it feels so good to be living on my own.

September 2004

Just when I thought everything was going smoothly on the legal side of the flat purchase, I feel as if I have been hit in the stomach.

I have been told by the Housing Trust more than once that the contracts *will* and *must* be exchanged by next Monday,

13 September. Not knowing how these things work, I gave my solicitors a call. I should have received some papers to sign by now. It came as a hell of a shock to learn that he'd sent the papers to the Trust's solicitors two weeks ago and nothing has been returned. I felt winded and panicky – the deadline is less than a week away.

I called my contact at the Housing Trust straight away and she assured me that she would phone their solicitors and demand that they send the paperwork back immediately. She also urged me not to worry and that the contracts would be exchanged next Wednesday – no ifs, no buts.

OK, I'll try to stop worrying. Anyway, it's Friday now so there's nothing else I can do.

☆ ☆ ☆ ☆ ☆ ☆

Things are actually moving – I received a letter with a pile of papers from my solicitors.

☆ ☆ ☆ ☆ ☆ ☆

I can't believe it! I just had another shock! And this one is a biggie! It's Friday, 10 September and my solicitor is blithely informing me that on Monday I need to pay a 10% deposit on signature of the contract. And I have only just found this out! I do not have arrangements in place to transfer funds so quickly. What am I going to do?!

OK, first thing – *don't panic!* I have arranged for my savings account funds to be transferred to my current account and they assured me that they will be available on Tuesday, 9:00. I don't know whether or not to believe them so I just called my solicitor and he said that that would be all right so we changed the appointment from Monday, 13 September 4:30pm to the day after, Tuesday, 8:30am.

All I can think of is – it's not much longer to go; I'm nearly there.

☆ ☆ ☆ ☆ ☆ ☆

Today is Tuesday, 14 September and I've just come back to the office having first been to see my solicitors. Today was the conclusion of a process that started – actually, I don't remember exactly when I first began to accept that my relationship with Jim was over. It's been less than two years yet it feels as if it had been going on for much, much longer.

Even sitting there at my solicitor's office I felt numb, as if everything were unreal. I had to sign a pile of papers but, for some reason that I can't understand I became really stroppy and difficult. I refused to sign anything that referred to me as Susan Plumtree. I have not been Susan for several decades and I decided I was not about to start now. So the poor man had to change and initial piles and piles of sheets showing that name before I was prepared to sign.

Anyway, I'm now here, at the office, and still feeling numb – although it's now beginning to wear off.

This is the most incredible milestone for me: the end of a major stage in my life and the beginning of a new one.

October 2004

I feel as if I've had a life time's worth of experience since I first moved into my rented flat and yet it's only been about four and a half months. I've learned lots of new things about living on my own. Most importantly, emotionally it's the best experience of all. I'd made my little guest room in the house in Welwyn Garden City my home but, with Jim's energy permeating everything, I really couldn't make a difference or counteract the effects.

Living in my present flat, however, is altogether different. I have created a welcoming and loving place. Even though I never pretended to myself that this was anything other than temporary, I've still tended to think of it as home and, while I'm very happy here, I know I'm not going to miss it.

I've noticed that I'm rarely thinking about my new home, that is, I'm not living in the future. For the next week and a half this is still home. It's also one of the clearest experiences I've ever had of what it means to "be in the here and now".

☆ ☆ ☆ ☆ ☆ ☆

Ros, who also recently moved into a new flat, says she has more furniture than she needs and would I please (she actually said "please") take her dinner table and four chairs. They are really beautiful and fit the space in my new home to perfection. I have now arranged for auctioneers to remove mine.

☆ ☆ ☆ ☆ ☆ ☆

It's Sunday evening. Not long to go now – just three days.

I'd been planning to do all kinds of things over my last weekend here but I came down with a heavy cold.

At first I thought, "the timing really stinks" but, on reflection, and strange as it may sound, I've come to see it as a real bonus. I feel fuzzy and weak, quite apart from sneezing and streaming, so I have simply stopped. I can't even be bothered to fret about last minute things. Anyway, I've done the best that I could to prepare for the move and there's nothing more I can do at this stage which would make any difference. I've decided to settle down and take it easy.

Actually, I'll go even further. This move has been planned with military precision – so there's nothing left to do. My active part was to note down a few commonsense tasks but the way it actually happened was that ideas would come into my head and I'd think "that's a really good idea! Thanks!" and then do it; then another one would pop up – and things just flowed.

Despite the cold I will definitely go to work tomorrow and Tuesday, as planned. The auctioneers have removed the table, chairs and coffee table. The coffee table was a last minute decision. It's very "Seventies" and doesn't feel right anymore. Now these things have gone, the flat has lost its "homey" feel so I'd rather not be here.

Tomorrow evening I'll be saying goodbye to some of the neighbours who have been very kind and helpful.

I'm actually looking forward to the move – Wednesday will be incredibly busy and I know I will be exhausted by the evening. The great thing is that Andrea has offered to prepare me a hot meal once the move is done, a wonderful way of ending such an important and life-changing day.

On Thursday, Toria (she of "how hard can it be?" fame) is coming in the morning and we'll be spending the day together unpacking and sorting things out. And, finally, on Saturday, I'll be meeting another friend for lunch. Throughout this period there will be several deliveries so the level of activity will be high. Friday and Sunday I will be on my own in my new home. That is really special. In fact, it's all special.

☆ ☆ ☆ ☆ ☆ ☆

I was so keyed up that I woke earlier than I'd hoped and yet it gave me time and space to do things without having to rush, including my morning meditation.

Eamonn (the removal man) and his crew arrived pretty much on time and got on with it. My job (which I didn't always live up to) was to stay out of their way. They were a joy to watch, approaching their task with total professionalism and care while displaying a great sense of humour. Eamonn really cares about all his clients and that includes me. Since the previous Sunday I'd gone down with a really heavy cold and virtually lost my voice. My energy levels were low but my spirits were high. At one point I noticed that, by mistake, my coat had been packed away so I croaked, "Eamonn, if I get a cold it'll be your fault!" He laughed, but ten minutes later he came over and put his own jacket around my shoulders.

Later that morning the cleaners arrived. The flat had been handed to me in a meticulous condition and it was very important to me to hand it back in the same state. I also wanted my full deposit back.

Completion, with the formal handover of the keys by Marie at the Housing Trust, was at 2:00 PM and there were certain formalities to observe. When we met outside she opened the front door and then handed me the keys to my new home for me to do the honours. I felt so emotional. I asked her teasingly, "Are you going to carry me over the threshold?" and we both laughed.

The formalities over, Eamonn and his lads got to work. Halfway through I had to leave to do the inventory with my ex-landlady, take the final readings and so on. When I returned, Eamonn had plugged in my radio, the standard lamp and various other bits of equipment which made my new home feel instantly welcoming.

I didn't have a lot of time to savour the moment because I needed to get ready to go to Andrea's. The evening had turned chilly; it was dark and pouring with rain.

When I arrived at her place she threw the door open and hugged me, welcoming me with a broad smile. Inside, there was a "real" fire in the fireplace, the table was set and there was music playing in the background.

It was a very special evening and, afterwards, she drove me home. To be at the receiving end of such love is really something else.

☆ ☆ ☆ ☆ ☆ ☆

Yesterday evening, Friday, there was an unexpected call from Niki.

"How would you like to have a visit tomorrow?", she asked. I practically shouted into the phone "YES!!!" I can't believe I'm going to see her tomorrow. What a treat!

☆ ☆ ☆ ☆ ☆ ☆

I've just come back from seeing Niki off at the station. Where has the day gone? We spent six hours together yet it feels like half an hour.

When I showed her my new home she was struck by how good it looks and feels – even though it's only been a couple of days since I moved in. I was going to prepare a meal for her but she didn't want me to go to any trouble.

I explained, "You don't understand. My home is a place where people are nourished and where they feel loved, and my cooking is part of it."

That has been my intention all along. My home will be a place where people will feel happy – where they will feel loved and cherished – including myself.

I'm increasingly recognising that it's all to do with process, by which I mean how I do everything and anything. In the case of cooking, the process includes every stage of preparing the meal. That's what I noticed being with Andrea the other evening. When I arrived I felt enveloped by love. That's how I want my friends to feel when they come here.

☆ ☆ ☆ ☆ ☆ ☆

It's Saturday evening and really late. I was woken by sounds of fireworks because it's Halloween. I sat by the window gazing at beautiful fireworks and pretending they were for me – a joyous welcome into my new life.

☆ ☆ ☆ ☆ ☆ ☆

I can't believe it: I'm really home.

November 2004

The transition into my new life and new home have depleted my savings more than I had anticipated and I now have much less money left for furnishing my flat than I'd thought.

In fact, it is a blessing in disguise because I have been very impatient to have my flat all sorted by Christmas – which is less than seven weeks away. Niki has been urging me to slow down and "get to know" my flat and myself better first, so that I can gradually discover how to best arrange it to support my lifestyle. Having so much less money means that I'm forced to slow down – a good thing, as it turned out.

☆ ☆ ☆ ☆ ☆ ☆

This evening, on my return from a night out there was a major shock waiting for me: a letter from Richmond Council. I couldn't believe my eyes. My new council tax band had gone up from band C to band E – an increase of £137 per month.

At first I thought I had mis-read the letter. I thought, "no, this cannot be". I then decided that what I really wanted to do is go to sleep because I felt tired and couldn't think straight.

I was getting ready to go to bed and having all these thoughts going round and round in my head along the lines of how I was going to handle what I regarded as "the impossible". Then I thought, "no, it's not impossible, I know I will be able to handle it." I then went to bed and slept really well.

As I woke up I was aware that that Knowing – that I would be able to handle the challenge – was still there. And, unusually for me in the context of money, I feel totally at peace.

☆ ☆ ☆ ☆ ☆

I have just read through my previous entry and was struck by my choice of words, "I know I will be able to handle it." In the past I used those very words to refer to my strength, being a "hero", not needing anyone. So much struggle! This time the words are the same but the meaning is completely different. This time I use these words to mean that I trust myself and that I will be alright. The sensation in my body is also completely different. Before, when I used the term "I can handle it" my body felt tight ready to fight or flee. Now, when I use it, my body feels light and relaxed.

☆ ☆ ☆ ☆ ☆

I'm still experiencing inner peace. However, my back pain has returned with a vengeance. Thank goodness for painkillers.

☆ ☆ ☆ ☆ ☆

My back pain has worsened. Nights are particularly bad. I haven't been able to get much sleep for over a week now and the other day I reached the point where I just stood there, in the middle of Sainsbury's, totally unable to move and fighting hard not to burst into tears. I now won't go anywhere without painkillers and a bottle of water. The problem is that I often don't see it coming until it's too late.

☆ ☆ ☆ ☆ ☆

This is no way to live. If there's one thing I've learned, though, it is that the situation is not hopeless and I am not impotent to do anything about – whatever. Right now, my "whatever" happens to be my backache. I have just called Aarti Shah, the McTimoney chiropractor I used last time my back pain was really bad. She did her magic on me two years ago and it lasted until now. I left her a message on her voicemail and when she called me back she said I sounded desperate – and I was. We made an appointment for Friday.

December 2004

I have now had two sessions with her and the difference has been immeasurable.

I also took a further step. I made a major investment in myself and bought a new bed frame and mattress. It was long overdue but nothing had caused me – until now – to consider doing it.

Thank goodness Ros came along with me or else I would have been unable to go through with it when I realised just how much it cost. I have never spent so much money on myself before.

I now have to wait six weeks for delivery but at least I know that this will give me restful nights.

☆ ☆ ☆ ☆ ☆ ☆

The year is coming to an end and, looking back, I feel as if I've lived a year and a half all packed into one.

I also have a feeling of completeness, of having reached the end of a major stage in my life and an awareness that, since all endings are, at the same time, new beginnings, a sense of expectancy and excitement and openness to whatever life will send me next.

And there's also this little voice whispering in my ear: "the best is yet to come!".

☆ ☆ ☆ ☆ ☆ ☆

I will be sixty in less than two months. I keep thinking about this, trying to work out what it means to me. About six months ago, in the context of Pete's 30th birthday, I remember teasing him, and suddenly and unexpectedly feeling intensely vulnerable. I knew that the reason was partly because, socially speaking, it is such a significant milestone, especially for women because it is the age when women receive their State pension, many stop working and are officially declared "old". There was a time, not all that long ago, when the State pension was actually called "old age pension". People receiving that pension were "pensioners", a term that goes beyond the factual interpretation of a person who is in receipt of a pension. The word "pensioner" conjures up someone who no longer makes a contribution to life, who is retired from participating in the world – except as a grandparent whose role is to babysit and spoil their grandchildren.

I actually don't care about what reaching sixty means in "social" terms. I'm trying to figure out what it means to me personally and all I can come up with is – nothing. Over the last few years, I've been becoming more self-aware and I've begun to understand that age milestones tend to have a deep psychological impact. I'm witnessing this in Pete and Will who have both turned thirty within a couple of months of each other. They're both wondering, as I am, how they should be feeling or they compare themselves with their younger friends and feel different – more "grown up". At least, that's what they tell me.

Will has a terrific relationship with his Dad – more like friends – and they like to do all kinds of things together. So Will doesn't have an "older" role model and, I now realise, nor do I.

My friends range from mid-twenties, mid-thirties, mid-forties to a couple within my age range but I'm wondering if I should feel something – I just don't know what. I also know I shouldn't think in terms of "should".

I don't want to pretend that I'm not growing older; otherwise, I'll wake up one day and die of shock except I still don't know what I mean by "not pretending".

☆ ☆ ☆ ☆ ☆ ☆

I really don't know what's going on. I've been feeling really weepie and I don't know why. My thoughts are all over the place. I don't think it has anything to do with turning sixty but I've been spending an enormous amount of time thinking "I don't want to be on my own around my birthday period." I suspect though that this is a distraction from something else.

I've been having flashbacks of incidents from my life with Jim which are intensely painful. Why should this come up now?

"I've been alone long enough" is also a thought which keeps popping up. When Ros asked me what I meant by that I had to admit that I didn't really know. I've felt alone throughout most of my life with Jim but I don't really feel alone now. If I were to be really honest with myself, I'm scared that I will never know what it's really like to love and to be loved.

☆ ☆ ☆ ☆ ☆ ☆

I'm having this rather odd feeling of aimlessness. I spent the last two years living with an intense and unwavering determination of going for my freedom and a home of my own – and now that I've achieved both I have this sense of "and now, what?"

Actually, there still is a lot to do – I haven't furnished my home yet. I'm sort of making friends with my flat first, rather than rushing in, trying to get everything ready before I myself am ready and more "at one" with the atmosphere and its own energy. I am only just beginning to feel ready to hang my pictures. I am not the least bit impatient. My home feels like my home, just as it is, even with very little furniture.

I am happy to give myself the time and the space to consolidate. I've been living on my own for just under eight months and in my own flat for only three – which is no time at all.

And, judging from my comments the other day, I'm still processing old hurts which I know is a vital and productive thing to do.

Meanwhile, I'm going out with friends, planning my landmark birthday, also a fantastic holiday later this year in Greece, signing up for workshops, doing all kinds of things. I'm not exactly twiddling my thumbs.

☆ ☆ ☆ ☆ ☆ ☆

I have finally, after a lot of struggling, resisting and chasing red herrings, recognised what this empty feeling actually is: I still feel lonely. I didn't want to see it because it seemed so ungrateful (I can't believe I'm saying this).

It also is a different loneliness to the way I used to feel when I was with Jim. Then I would tell myself that I'm feeling lonely *because* he doesn't listen to me, doesn't let me share my life with him, won't share his with me. Now that I don't have him to blame anymore, there is nowhere to hide. I just feel lonely.

☆ ☆ ☆ ☆ ☆ ☆

I can't believe how much I'm looking forward to my birthday. I've always loved birthdays and this one is no exception – now that I've got my brain around the whole idea of turning sixty.

There are all kinds of treats planned – on my own as well as with friends and my team mates here at work.

☆ ☆ ☆ ☆ ☆ ☆

Today, 17 March, felt very powerful – it was the last day of my Fifties. What a thought! More than that – it was one hell of a decade when I, and therefore my whole life, changed from the bottom up – beyond recognition.

I also had a wonderful day, with all of it feeling so good – a great way to end this stage of my life. Now I feel ready for the next one.

☆ ☆ ☆ ☆ ☆ ☆

This has been the best birthday I have ever had, spending time with the people I love the most.

I noticed this morning that I'm experiencing a wonderful sense of ease with myself: I like who I have become and am in the process of becoming. I like my new tendency to keep pushing back the limits of my comfort zone moving into new territory, experimenting, taking risks, acknowledging it when I feel scared, full of doubt or fear yet staying with it. I like it that I no longer – or rarely – pretend (to myself and others) that I feel one thing when I actually feel another, admit when I feel vulnerable, try to notice when I let myself down and retrace my steps without beating myself up – too much, anyway.

I now can accept that it is alright to revisit old habits, old fears, the occasional lonely feeling. It is all part of my being human.

I have no idea what life will bring – but I'm willing to deal with whatever that might be with as much grace and courage as I can muster. And when I don't live up to this hope then I know I have friends who will gently tap me on the shoulder and help me notice. And, of course, there's Alan who has been with me throughout this journey and, I hope, will come along for the next stage of my life.

I think that my greatest achievement so far is to aim to be as fully human as I know how – acknowledging all my great qualities as well as the ones I'd rather not have – but do. It's what makes me whole and real and that, to me, is what matters most.

EPILOGUE

Over the last three years, since my narrative ended, my life has changed beyond recognition. Not only mine but Jim's as well.

He moved to a small town overseas and established himself as a campaigner in environmental matters specialising in time-related issues in the context of energy savings and climate change. He keeps me informed about his progress and setbacks and I, in turn, tell him how proud I am of him. He sounds happy and fulfilled.

As for me, after seven years working as a Client Development Executive, a job I thoroughly enjoyed for the first six years, I finally decided to leave. I just had to follow my heart's calling and now work full time as a coach and mentor. I continue to write and I'm currently working on my next book. I also facilitate workshops and give interactive talks. I am where I belong.

These past three years have taught me the extent to which I have learned to trust myself, particularly when my inner voice tells me it's time to move while my fears try to keep me from flying to new heights, as they have always tried to do. The difference now is that I recognise them to be part of a forward moving process, although admittedly it has rarely been a case of "feeling the fear and doing it anyway." As I look back to how I keep being propelled forwards to the next stage of my life I see that nothing can shift as long as I'm in the grip of fear.

My process involves moving from fear to clarity and from clarity to action. And I also learned that it is a process that takes as long as it takes.

As I'm writing this I sense I am, again, at the threshold of a new stage of my life but I have no idea what it will look like. I only know that it will be exciting and that I'm up to the challenge, whatever that challenge might be. To me, this is a wonderful way to live.

Sue Plumtree

Flat 10 – Floyer Close
Queen's Road
Richmond, Surrey TW10 6HS

Tel. 020 8940 7056
Email sue@sueplumtree.co.uk
Website www.sueplumtree.co.uk